SPOOKY SCIENCE

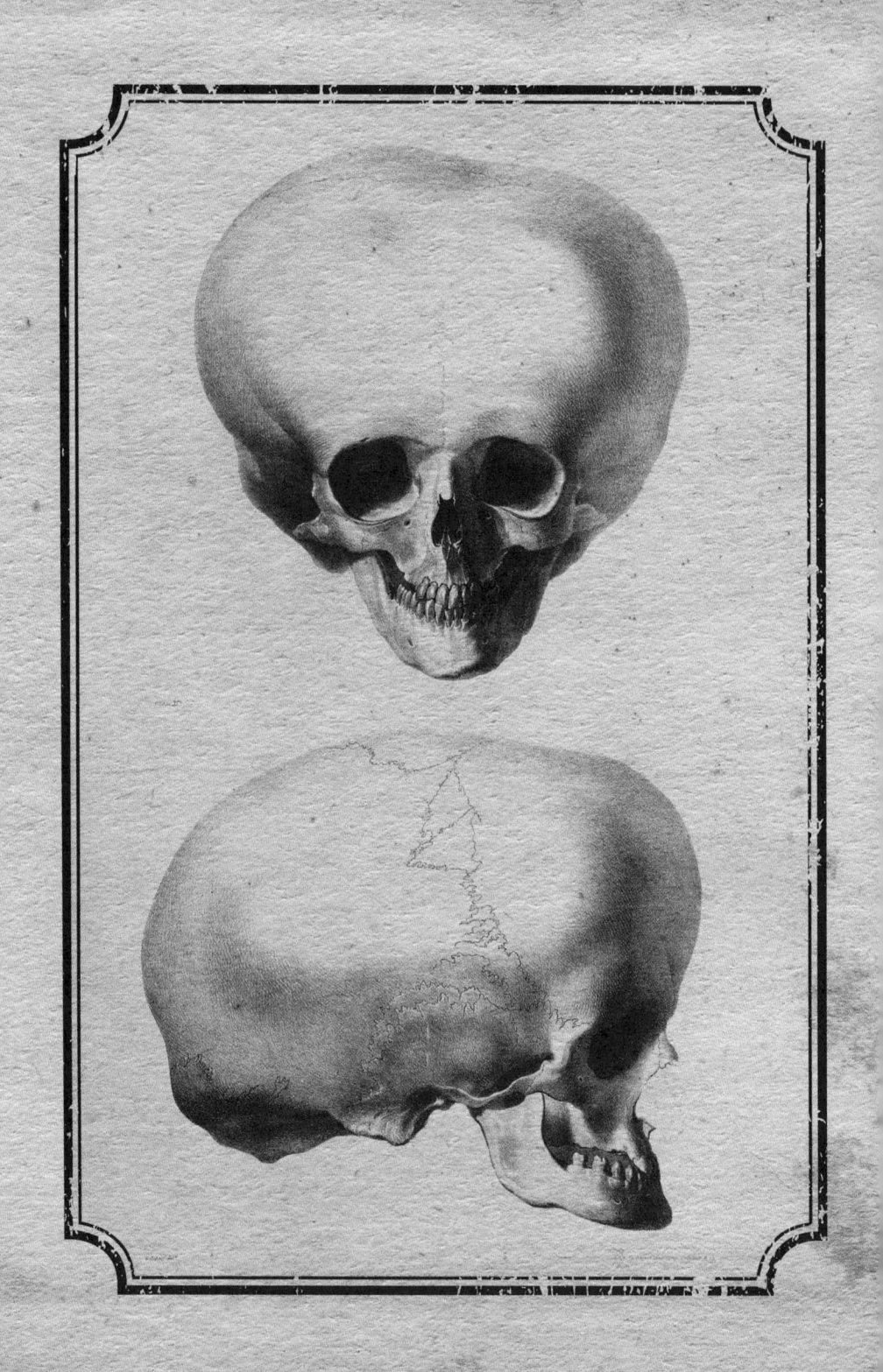

SPOOKY SCIENCE

❖❖❖❖❖❖❖

DISSECTING THE MYSTERIES OF GHOSTS, CRYPTIDS, ALIENS, AND OTHER ODDITIES

❖❖

MEAGAN ANKNEY

PAIGE MILLER

CREATORS OF SPOOKY SCIENCE SISTERS

castle

CONTENTS

Introduction ❖ 7

A Note on the Scientific Method
and the Paranormal ❖ 14

Part I: Things That Go "Boo!" in the Night ❖ 19
A Brief History of Ghosts and the Afterlife ❖ 20
The Science of Ghost Encounters ❖ 32
The "Science" of Paranormal Investigation ❖ 57

**Part II: Creepy Creatures and
Legendary Features ❖ 73**
Monsters ❖ 75
Cryptids ❖ 105
Urban Legends ❖ 139
Aliens ❖ 161

Conclusion ❖ 197

Test Your Knowledge Answer Key ❖ 199

Selected Bibliography ❖ 204
Index ❖ 206
Acknowledgments ❖ 210
About the Authors ❖ 211

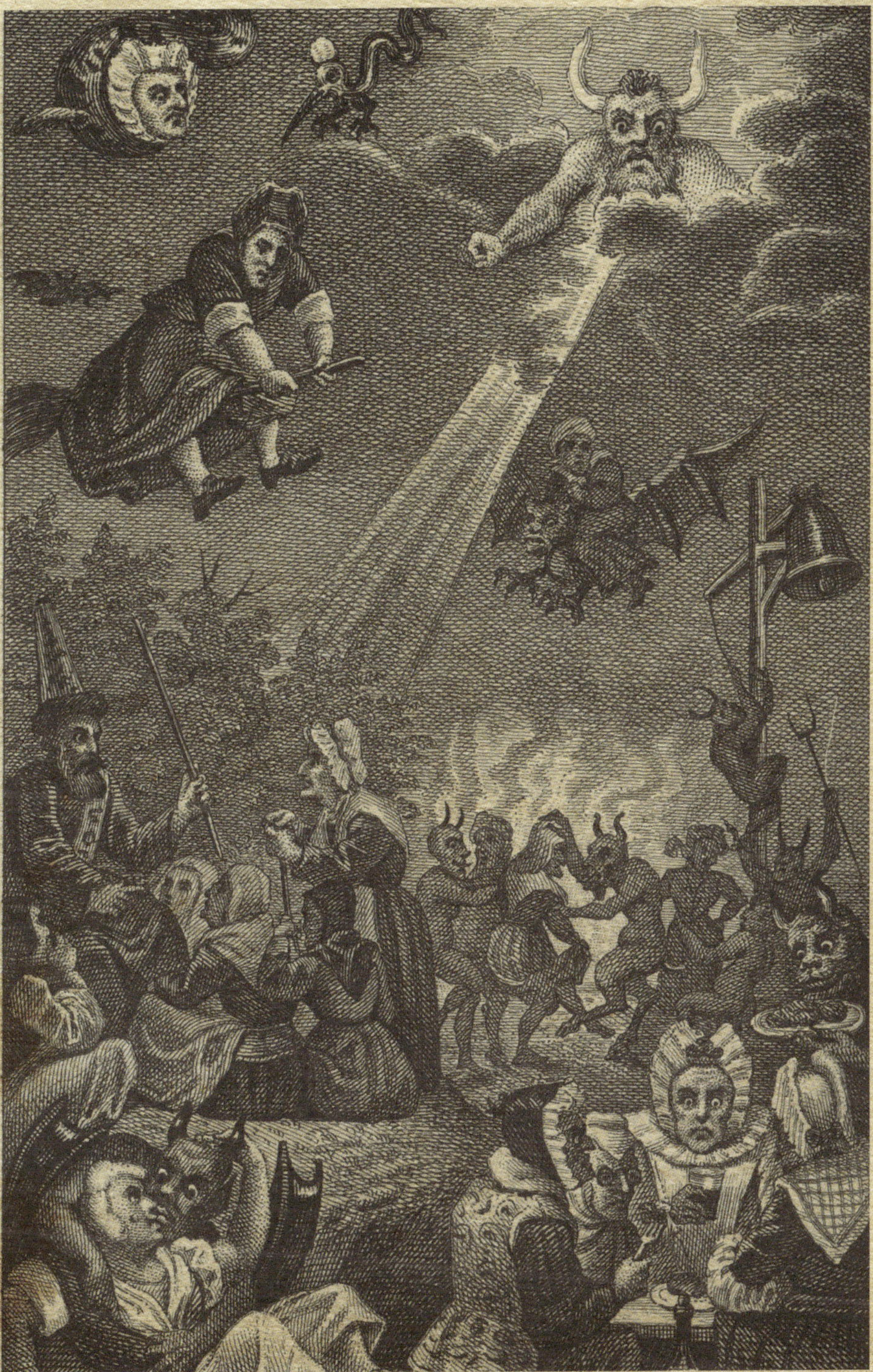

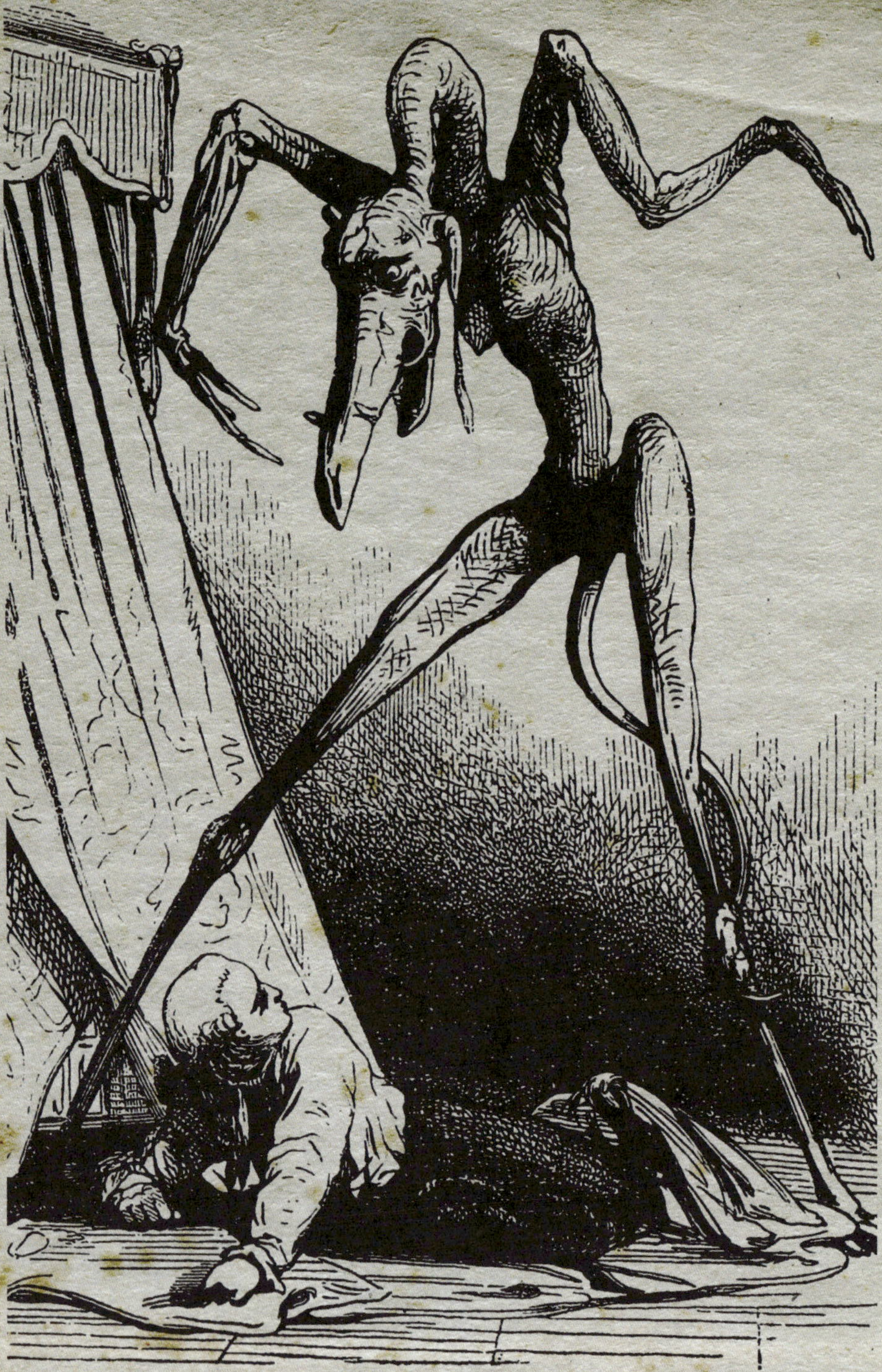

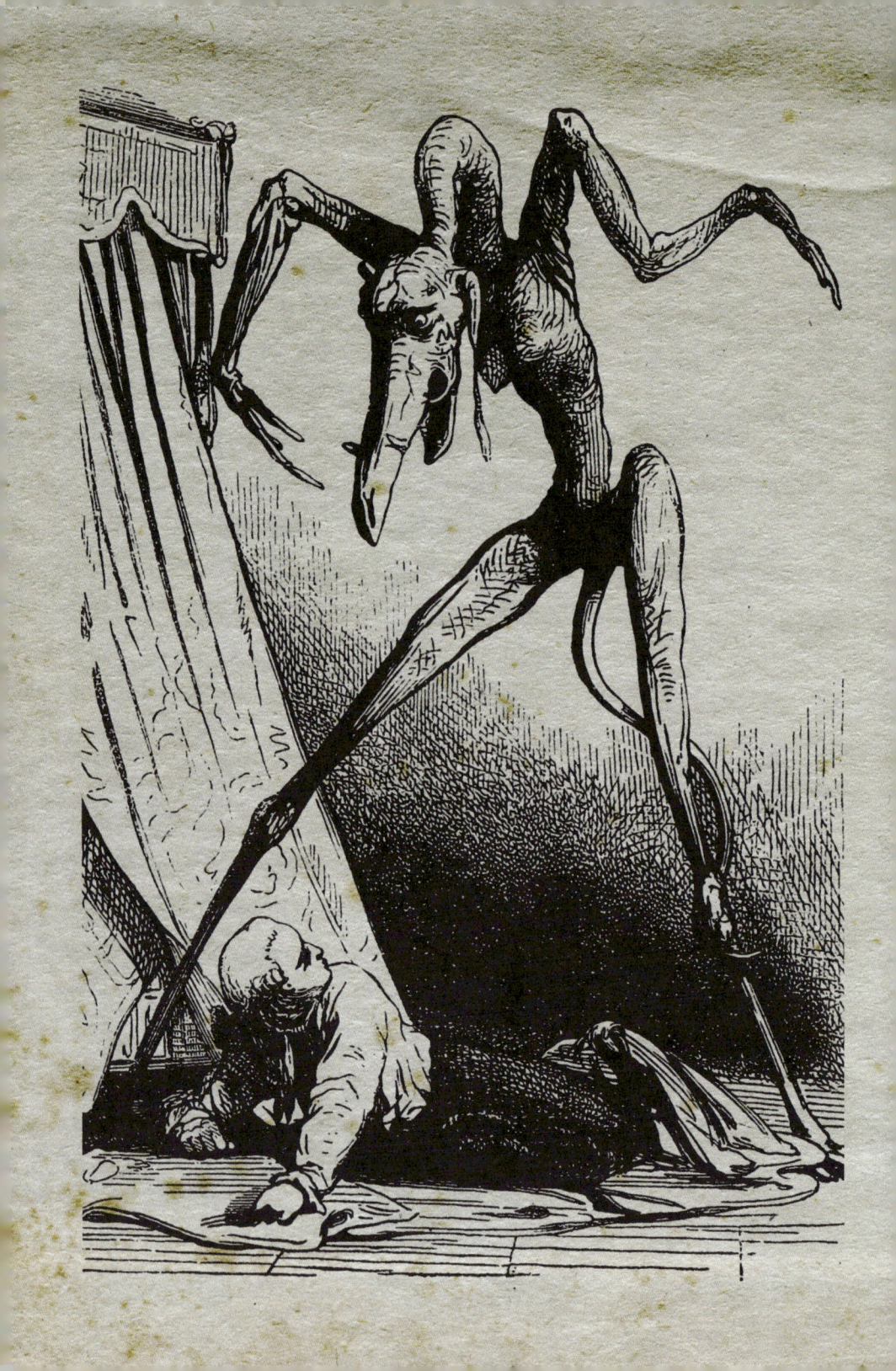

INTRODUCTION

IT STARTED WITH A FLUKE...

I can remember the exact timing of my first brush with spooky science. It was 9 p.m. in late September 1994, and almost-seven-year-old me was thrilled that I had successfully convinced my parents to allow me to stay up late enough to watch *The X-Files* with them. In their defense, it was a Friday night, and I had already survived an in-theater viewing of *Jurassic Park* when I was five years old. That night, an episode titled "The Host" (episode 2, season 2) aired, wherein a half-fluke, half-man that has escaped from the radioactive bilge water of a Russian cargo ship squeezes out of people's toilets and drains to attack and eat them.

Unsurprisingly, I was left absolutely terrified. I remember asking my mom if flukes were real and was horrified when, without hesitation, she told me that yes, flukes (a class of parasitic flatworms) are real and incredibly common. She of course assured me that they were very small, but finding out that this terrifying monster story had an aspect of truth to it left a lasting impression. Let me be the first to admit that I spent the next several years convinced that I might be attacked by a monstrous wormlike creature every time I used the bathroom.

... AND NOW I'M MAKING IT EVERYONE ELSE'S PROBLEM

Flash forward to March 2020, and I, like most of the world, was stuck at home and looking for something to distract myself from the fear and uncertainty of the early days of the COVID-19 pandemic. For me, that came in the form of playing an obscene number of hours of *Animal Crossing* but also keeping myself company by listening to my favorite podcasts. A couple of weeks into this new (not-so-) normal, and I, like many (probably delusional) podcast listeners before me, decided, "Hey, I can do this too!"

Of course, I couldn't do it alone. Luckily, I am blessed with an amazing sister-in-law, Paige, whose severe case of FOMO (fear of missing out) prevents her from saying no to anything, and thus, with a cohost acquired, *Spooky Science Sisters* was born. Now, five years in, and almost one hundred episodes later, Paige and I (along with many expert guests) have discussed a wide variety of spooky and strange topics ranging from ghosts to bigfoot to aliens to massive volcanic eruptions. What sets us apart from most podcasts that delve into paranormal phenomena, however, is that we do so from a scientific, or skeptical, perspective.

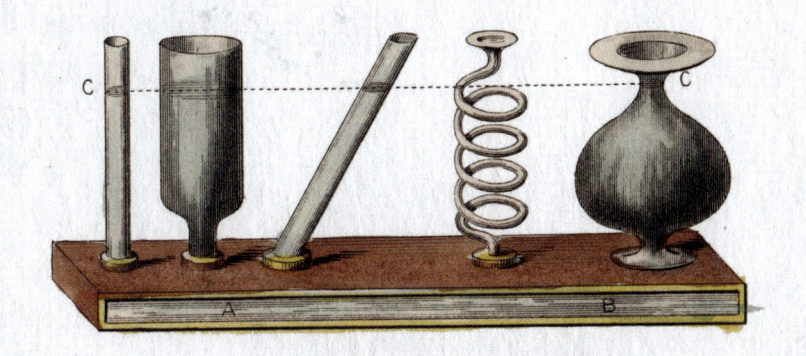

HOW THIS BOOK WORKS

Spooky Science is divided into two main parts and contains detailed examinations of five paranormal phenomena. For each topic, Paige and I will tell you about its historical and folkloric origins, and then we'll take a look at possible logical and scientific explanations. Part I is all about ghosts, and Part II covers additional supernatural phenomena, namely monsters, cryptids, urban legends, and aliens.

You'll likely notice that this setup means we've allotted a bit more space to ghosts relative to other topics. This is partly because ghosts are such a huge and widely studied topic, even in the scientific community. But also, many of the psychiatric and environmental factors that we discuss in detail in "The Science of Ghost Encounters" (page 32) are able to be more briefly revisited throughout the book in relation to other supernatural phenomena. For each of the sections in Part II, we selected examples that we felt were representative of each genre and that cover a range of possible scientific explanations.

The main text of *Spooky Science* was written by Meagan. Throughout the book, you'll also encounter sidebars with additional details, an extra story, or other information about a given topic. These sidebars are where you'll find Paige (page 11). There are also two special sidebar features that you'll come across in each of the five sections. The first are Test Your Knowledge sidebars with quiz questions based on the themes of each section. Don't worry—you'll also be given the answers, which might be things we've covered in the main text or other supernatural stories we love! The other special type of sidebar is a nod to one of our favorite segments on the podcast, "Something Spooky." In each of these sidebars we share a personal anecdote related to the spooky phenomena being discussed in the main text.

"Hello!"
From the Second Sister

As a child I always looked forward to Halloween and listening to a good campfire ghost story. But my long-standing fascination with horror and the paranormal really began when I opened my copy of *Coraline*—a book that introduced me to a more mature version of horror. In the last twenty years I've spent countless hours watching, reading, and listening to spooky stories. A portion of my teenage years were spent exploring "haunted" buildings, bridges, and parks, doing my own amateur version of ghost hunting.

In my many tours of supposedly haunted locations, I've had no encounters with apparitions and no ghostly photographs, and I've not had any experiences I couldn't explain. The only notably strange experience I've had was discovering my brother and I had the same imaginary friend, six years apart (you'll read more about this later on page 102).

As my years without one of these experiences continued, and my interest in the natural sciences evolved, I became increasingly more skeptical of the possibilities of a supernatural world. As an adult, I've learned that the natural world and the things our brains do to trick us are often more terrifying than any supernatural explanation. I still enjoy the thrill of exploring allegedly haunted places and hearing stories of the paranormal, and I will never turn down the opportunity to watch a ghost hunting show. But now I find enjoyment in thinking through and researching the psychological and scientific phenomena at play.

THE SPIRIT OF SPOOKY SCIENCE

Examining paranormal phenomena through a scientific lens is often a tricky proposition. There is certainly a stigma that exists within the academic community that researching the paranormal is unserious and not a worthwhile pursuit. Although I do not necessarily agree with this viewpoint, as a scientist and a naturally skeptical person myself, I understand where it comes from. At a fundamental level, investigating supernatural phenomena that, by definition, fall outside of the theoretical framework of what is known about the natural world is just not possible. You cannot form or reliably test a hypothesis about something that does not follow the laws of physics or biology or whatever the relevant branch of science may be.

While there are scientists out there doing the work to appropriately apply the scientific method to the paranormal, it is typically in the form of testing mechanisms by which the human brain might trick itself into believing something paranormal has occurred. Understandably, this approach then leads to frustration and defensiveness directed toward mainstream science within the paranormal community. Much of the paranormal is rooted in personal experiences and beliefs, and it is difficult to have someone tell you that what you saw or experienced, which you felt was profoundly important, was a misunderstanding, a trick of the mind, or a hoax. Unfortunately, this means that many believers end up turning to "experts" whose investigations into the paranormal fall firmly in the realm of pseudoscience, and that is a difficult rabbit hole to climb out of.

Because of these difficulties, I don't think anyone, skeptic or believer, will ever be able to give a definitive answer as to the existence of most, if not all, paranormal phenomena, or at least one that would satisfy both parties. The exceptions, of course, are if someone actually manages to drag a bigfoot corpse out of the woods or produce a crashed alien spacecraft, but so far, those seem like unlikely possibilities. And believe me, I *know* the ambiguity is frustrating. All I can offer you is my own opinion, backed by a lifetime of interest in the paranormal and five years spent researching and discussing it from a scientific viewpoint, that the evidence isn't there to support the existence of any of the paranormal topics we'll cover in this book, at least in the literal sense, and at least *for now*.

That said, being skeptical doesn't mean I am any less fond of the supernatural, and it is not my goal here to convince anyone that they shouldn't believe in the paranormal. Telling stories about ghosts and monsters and other strange phenomena is an essential part of being human. Ghost stories help people cope with the uncertainty of death and the pain of grief. Monster stories have long been a way for society to contextualize fears about current events or explain natural phenomena that people don't understand. Following World War II and the subsequent boom of technology leading to the space race, our fears took to the sky, manifesting as otherworldly visitors. In that sense, paranormal phenomena are real because they serve a real, and important, purpose in our lives, and have done so for millennia. That is the spirit we embrace and they hope to share with you throughout the pages of *Spooky Science*.

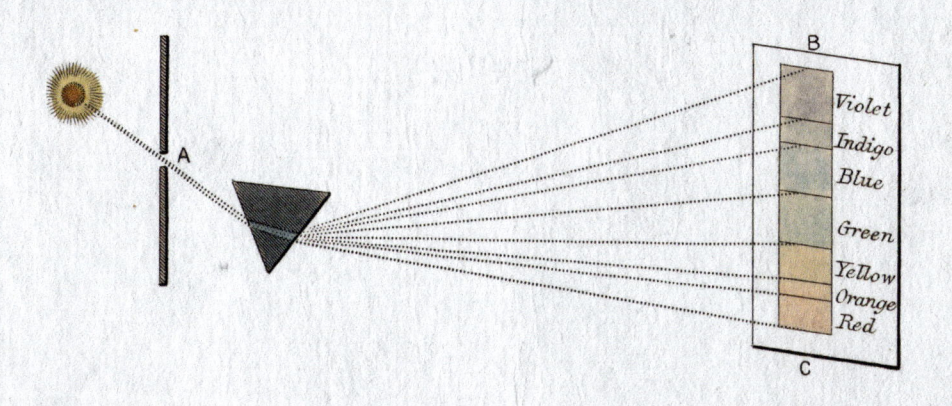

A Note on the Scientific Method and the Paranormal

One of the most important characteristics of science is that it isn't a set of facts or a "thing" to be believed or held up as absolute truth. Science is better thought of as a method, or tool, for learning about the world. Paranormal investigations, on the other hand, often fall into the realm of pseudoscience (or "false science"), meaning that they look (or pretend to be) scientific from the outside but are fundamentally incompatible with the principles laid out by the scientific method. So, what is the scientific method, and what are some of the ways that pseudoscience and paranormal research fall short? Let's review:

1. The scientific method starts with making observations that are based on or used to determine a question you'd like to investigate. In general, this question should seek to build upon or refine our current understanding of the natural world and assumes the natural world behaves in measurable, repeatable ways.

    Many paranormal phenomena, by definition, already do not meet these criteria.

2. The next step is to form a hypothesis, which is a tentative explanation for whatever phenomenon you set out to investigate.

This hypothesis must be testable, meaning that it is possible to conduct experiments that will either support or refute it. A key aspect of this is that being able to disprove, or falsify, your hypothesis is just as important as being able to find evidence that it is correct. Basically, to know what something is, you also have to be able to conclusively find out what it isn't, and in science, that means you have to be able to measure it.

A hypothesis is untestable and/or unfalsifiable when:

- It is based on a matter of opinion, or is subjective. For example, Bigfoot is a better cryptid than Nessie. What is "better"? How do you measure it?

- The technology to test it doesn't exist, and/or there is no feasible way to design an experiment to do so. Let's say your hypothesis is that haunted houses are more active when the ghosts that live there are angry. One way to demonstrate this could be measuring ghost activity in haunted houses with angry ghosts and not-angry ghosts. But no scientific instruments exist that are known to measure ghosts, their activity levels, or their level of anger (and yes, I can already hear some of you asking about ghost-hunting equipment that is claimed to be scientific—I promise we'll come back to it).

- It is overly vague or broad. This is the realm in which psychics, astrology, and metaphysics operate. You might hypothesize that a certain type of crystal attracts positive energy, but **(A)** "positive energy" is not a measurable thing, and **(B)** it is too vague.

- The goal posts are continually moved, as is often the case with paranormal phenomena.

You might claim that a house is haunted, but when someone investigates and finds no evidence of ghosts, then perhaps it's only certain people who are "open-minded" enough to sense them, or the ghosts were scared off by the equipment that was brought in. There's always an excuse and the hypothesis can never be falsified.

3. Time to experiment! Test your hypothesis by gathering and analyzing data. Some considerations:

- Collecting data means not only looking for evidence that supports your hypothesis, but also investigating and ruling out every possible avenue that could show your hypothesis is wrong. Only looking for and recording data that supports your hypothesis is not objective (or free from bias) and is often the status quo for paranormal investigations.

- In a realistic scientific setting, you are often considering multiple hypotheses at once or frequently looping back around to form new ones as you rule others out.

- Personal anecdotes are not evidence. Memories were not collected under controlled circumstances, and they are not able to be replicated. There's also the matter of the fallibility of memory and perception, which we'll come back to in our discussion of the science of ghost encounters (page 32).

- Paranormal researchers are often searching for or recording anomalies, but without controls and baseline data, anomalies are meaningless. Actual scientific inquiry seeks to identify, monitor, and, if possible, eliminate sources of error. If a hypothesis is only supported by a few anomalous data points (meaning ones that are very different from the rest of a data set), rigorous testing is required to determine their validity, and they might suggest that a modified hypothesis is needed.

4. Now it's time to draw conclusions — was your hypothesis correct? If yes, move on to step five. If not, can you rule it out entirely and test a new one? Or can you modify it and test it again?

- Even if all other alternatives are ruled out, there is no such thing as absolute certainty that a hypothesis is true. There is only one that has not been demonstrated to be false. But if this happens often enough with respect to related hypotheses for a given phenomenon, you might have a scientific theory on your hands.

- Paranormal researchers often skip right to this step of the scientific method and work backwards. To put it simply, they are seeking confirmation for a foregone conclusion or belief and often ignore anything that doesn't support it.

5. Do it again and give others the information they need to do it again, too.

- Scientific studies must be replicable, meaning that when the experiments are repeated, the same results are obtained. This precludes many paranormal phenomena that cannot be reliably replicated (for example, random movements of doors in a "haunted" house).

- The body of scientific knowledge is always growing and changing as we learn more about the natural world, but that doesn't mean science is fickle. Change only happens after rigorous and repeated testing and peer review.

Having established these parameters, we are now ready to dive into the world of Spooky Science.

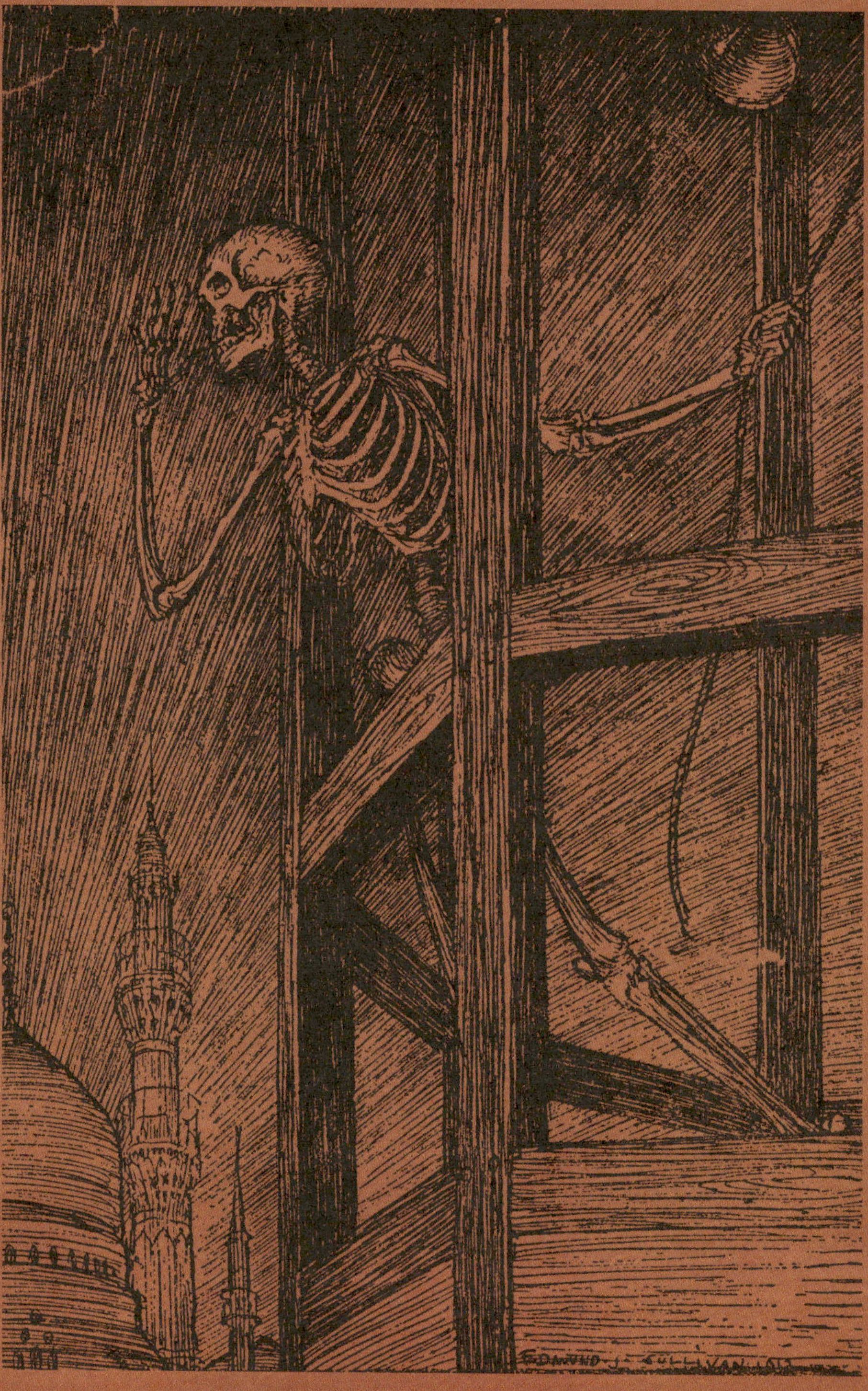
EDMUND J. SULLIVAN

PART I

THINGS THAT GO "BOO!" IN THE NIGHT

A BRIEF HISTORY OF GHOSTS AND THE AFTERLIFE

Humans are fascinated with the afterlife. Wondering what comes next after we depart this mortal plane is a fundamental part of what makes us human, and it only seems natural to consider that we don't end up that far away. And by that, of course, I mean that we become ghosts. It's perhaps not quite the paradise some are hoping for, but the introvert in me can certainly see the appeal of getting to stick around the places I'm familiar with. (Making friends is hard enough in the mortal world, I'm not trying to start over somewhere new.)

But when and where did the idea of ghosts come from in the first place, and what does science have to say about this nearly ubiquitous and enduring paranormal phenomenon? We know from archaeologists that the idea of ghosts is an ancient one, but before we get to that, we need to start more simply. Because to have ghosts, a society first has to believe in an afterlife, which also requires conceiving of a person as being more than just their physical body, meaning there must be some component of an individual that lives on after death. Belief in an afterlife, and possibly also ghosts, may go back tens of thousands of years, the first evidence of which can be found by looking at how our prehistoric ancestors disposed of and cared for their dead.

Prehistoric Ghosts: The Graves Are Good

Our timeline for belief in an afterlife begins in our prehistoric ancestors' graves. Deliberate burial of the dead began up to 130,000 years ago according to currently accepted archaeological evidence, and research into human evolution suggests that our species developed the mental capacity and language skills necessary to construct and communicate religious beliefs between groups at least sixty thousand years ago.

It's tough to say if these early burials were representative of any broader belief system or just for the sake of hygiene, but at the time they were happening, we know that our human ancestors were already using ochre pigments and creating decorative items such as beads, likely for symbolic reasons. A key marker of a belief in an afterlife may be when those decorative items started to show up as grave goods, which are objects that were intentionally buried alongside a deceased individual. In addition to decorative items including beads, jewelry, or pottery, grave goods could be practical things such as weapons, food, or money.

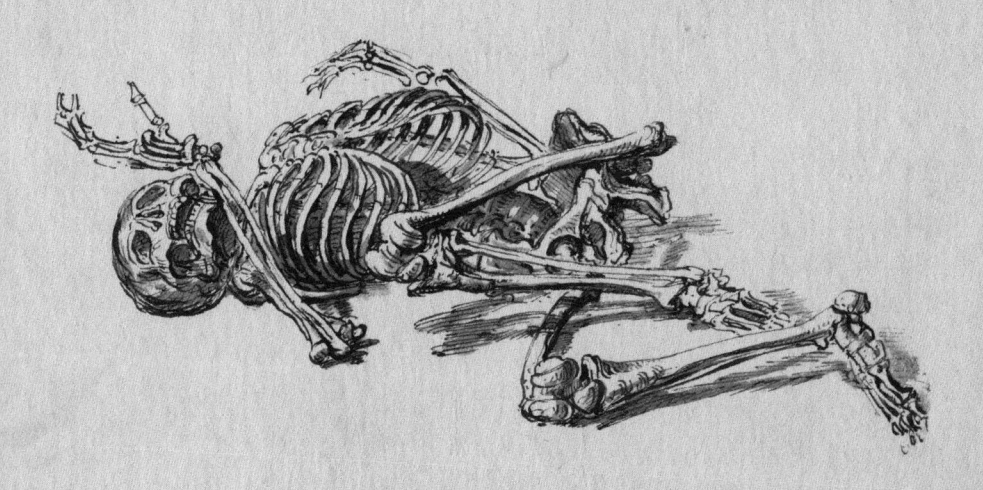

One of the best examples of prehistoric grave goods comes from a site known as Sunghir in Russia. It is there that the bodies of a man and two boys were excavated, and within their graves, archaeologists found spears along with several decorative objects, the most remarkable of which were strings of over thirteen thousand mammoth ivory beads. These three individuals were part of a group of hunter-gatherers who lived (and died) in the area around thirty-four thousand years ago. The ivory beads represent thousands of hours of manual labor, and in a hunter-gatherer society, spears would have held significant practical value. The presence of such elaborate grave goods suggests that this group of people had strong, complex cultural beliefs around the concept of death, which could be construed as religious beliefs or perhaps allude to a belief in an afterlife.

Animism and Ancestors: The Beginning of Ghosts

It's harder to pin down a time estimate of when the idea of ghosts was born, but it likely arose in relation to beliefs and customs associated with animism and the practice of ancestor worship. Animism purports that there is a spiritual force behind all things, including animals, plants, and nonliving objects, and in the context of conceptualizing the idea of ghosts, would allow that each person possesses their own spiritual essence, or what we would call a soul, that is distinct from their physical body.

Ancestor worship, or ancestor veneration, centers around the belief that deceased relatives continue their existence in some realm beyond the grave where they can observe, and sometimes interact with, the living. In many cases, it was believed that these ancestors had specific, and often ongoing, expectations of their living family. Failure to meet these expectations might result in a variety of undesirable outcomes. For example, an ancestor's soul could be trapped in the world of the living, unable to pass into the underworld, or could even choose to return to give their living relatives a piece of their mind. While some anthropologists have argued that the concept of ghosts is distinct from ancestors in this respect, it at least feels fair to suggest that it was an important step along the way.

MESOPOTAMIA: FROM THE CRADLE OF CIVILIZATION TO THE GRAVE

The first ghost stories in the historical record (so far) were produced around 4,300 years ago by the Sumerians of ancient Mesopotamia, who transcribed them in cuneiform (the oldest known form of writing) onto clay tablets. For the Mesopotamians, ghosts were a fact of life to be avoided or dealt with as needed. Writings from the Early Dynastic period of Mesopotamia (ca. 2900–2334 BCE) include spells for protection, exorcism ceremonies, and even summonings. Spirits could choose to come back to the physical world for several reasons, but troublesome ghosts returned due to:

1. Improper burial or insufficient veneration. The Mesopotamians kept their deceased relatives close, commonly burying them under the floors of their homes. The intention was that living relatives and descendants were never too far away to tend to their ancestors' graves.

2. Premature or violent death or dying with unfinished business. People who died under these conditions could come back as vengeful ghosts, tormenting the living, whom they resented.

Attracting the negative attention of either type of ghost could have dire consequences for the living, and this is where we get our first documented evidence of humans using ghosts to explain science they didn't understand yet, as many common ailments and diseases were blamed on the influence of an unhappy spirit.

Ancient Greece and Rome: How to Rent a Haunted House

Moving forward in time, the Greeks and the Romans were steeped in their own beliefs and stories about ghosts, but there is also evidence of skepticism to be found. Beliefs about the afterlife varied for both the Greeks and Romans, and thus there was disagreement as to whether ghosts existed at all. For example, the Epicureans, followers of the Greek philosopher Epicurus, did not believe in the existence of the soul after death, so ghosts were of no concern to them. Other Greek and Roman philosophers and scientists, such as Aristotle and Lucretius, also worked to find rational explanations for supposed supernatural or ghostly phenomena reported by their contemporaries.

A famous Roman author and politician, Pliny the Younger, wrote what many consider to be the most well-known ghost story of antiquity about a haunted house in Athens. In the story, a philosopher named Athenodorus knowingly rents a haunted house that has been left vacant after scaring away one too many tenants. Like so many horror movie homes of today, the rent on this house is unusually cheap, but brave Athenodorus can't pass up a deal and the chance to meet a ghost. Once he is settled, he soon encounters the terrifying, shackled apparition of an emaciated old man.

Initially, the intrepid philosopher is unfazed by the ghost's chain-rattling antics, but Athenodorus is eventually convinced to follow his ghostly visitor out to the courtyard, where the specter abruptly disappears. Beneath the spot where the ghost vanished, a set of bones, shackled and chained, is exhumed. After the skeleton is given a proper burial, the house is no longer haunted, and unfortunately for those of us dying to know more about the origins of the mysterious skeleton, that's where the story ends. We also don't know if the story was a "true" anecdote passed on to Pliny, or if it was fiction intended to be commentary on the moral obligation to disclose defaults with a home before renting it out or the importance of approaching the supernatural in a rational way.

AMERICA THE HAUNTED

Across the Atlantic Ocean, Indigenous Peoples in North America, Central (Meso-) America, and South America also believed in ghosts. As in the rest of the ancient world, ancestor worship and animism influenced practices and beliefs associated with death and the afterlife, including any ghosts that might be encountered, and unique variations developed across the many tribal nations that existed.

In North America, the behavior of ghosts ranged from malevolent, and even deadly, to helpful. The Navajo people are commonly featured in texts about Indigenous ghosts, as they traditionally believed that most, if not all, persons left behind any negative or evil parts of their spirits in this world as ghosts, or chindi. Chindi were to be greatly feared, and special precautions were taken to avoid attracting them, including prompt disposal of a deceased person's possessions, abandoning their home, refusing to speak their name, and even removing any footprints left around their grave. From a scientific perspective, avoiding the grave and the deceased's possessions also seems like a smart, practical way to avoid any contagions that may have caused their death.

Indigenous Mesoamerican peoples, such as the Aztecs and the Mayans, held prominent festivals to honor the dead: Miccailhuitontli (Little Feast of the Dead, honoring children) and Miccailhuitl (Great Feast of the Dead, honoring adults) in the case of the Aztecs and Hanal Pixan for the Mayans. In both cultures, these festivals featured offerings of food to the deceased. The Aztecs gave particular consideration to the spirits of women who died in childbirth, who were venerated similarly to warriors who perished in battle. They were known as cihuateteo, meaning "divine women," and spent most of their days helping to escort the sun across the sky. On five days of the year, though, the cihuateteo could be found haunting crossroads, attempting to steal children, causing illness or insanity, and even seducing men into committing adultery (although I hope the men's wives rolled their eyes as hard as I did about that last one). These legends may have been the inspiration for Mexico's infamous weeping woman ghost, La Llorona.

THE INFLUENCE OF CHRISTIANITY: WHAT HAPPENS IN PURGATORY STAYS IN PURGATORY

◆◆◆

Jumping back across the pond, with the rise of Christianity in Europe, ideas about the afterlife and ghosts changed as the Roman Catholic Church worked to distance itself from pagan beliefs. Early on, some worked to reject entirely the idea of ghosts as the spirits of the dead. For example, St. Augustine, a bishop and theologian during the late fourth and early fifth centuries, validated the supernatural experiences people reported, but he attributed them to spiritual visions sent by angels or demons, not ghosts. (Quite the ironic turn of fate for St. Augustine that the lighthouse in his namesake city in Florida would come to be known as one of the "most haunted" locations in the United States.)

Despite St. Augustine's influential status in the Church, ghost stories continued to flourish within and without the growing Christian world. Most of the narratives that developed about medieval ghosts from a Christian perspective focused on those trapped in purgatory, an idea that was formally established by the Church at the time. In general, these stories were intended to reinforce the existence of purgatory as well as warn the living of the suffering they might face there if they strayed.

The Origins of the Jack-o'-Lantern

One of the most famous purgatory ghost stories comes from the early seventeenth century. I'm referring, of course, to the legend of Stingy Jack, more famously known as Jack-o'-Lantern. According to most popular versions of the legend, Jack was a drunkard or a blacksmith, or both, who managed to trick the devil (multiple times!) out of claiming his soul. When Jack finally died, however, his trickery meant that neither heaven nor hell wanted to take him, and his punishment was to wander the Earth in purgatory for eternity with nothing but a burning ember to light his way.

The detail about the burning ember intertwined Jack's story with Celtic and Scandinavian folklore about the ghostly origins of will-o'-the-wisps. Scientifically, these mysterious lights are thought to be produced either through the spontaneous ignition of pockets of marsh gas rich in methane, which produces a flame, or due to a chemiluminescent reaction of the gasses, which produces a faint, blue glow. Stingy Jack's story was also eventually linked to the Halloween tradition of carving pumpkins to light the way for trick or treaters and perhaps some wayward souls set loose from purgatory for the night.

Ghosts of the Victorian Era

Modern beliefs about and attitudes toward ghosts in the Western world quickly began to solidify during the Victorian era (ca. 1837–1901). The Victorians loved ghost stories and are often described as having a fascination with death and the afterlife.

Within the context of the time, however, that fascination came with good reason. High mortality rates, especially in children, made death a constant fixture of Victorian life, and it was certainly more visible than today, with the majority of deaths happening at home.

The United States also saw the death of over six hundred thousand people during the Civil War, which understandably left a scar on the American psyche and led to a desire to contact lost loved ones. And like any of the cultures we've talked about thus far, the Victorians had to establish their own set of customs and rituals to deal with these morbid realities.

Spiritualism: A Toe-Crackin' Ghost Time

Victorian mourning customs reflected the great economic changes, as well as rapid advances in science and technology, happening at the time. Some advances must have seemed almost supernatural, including inventions such as the telegraph, the telephone, movies, home electricity, and photography. And indeed, portrait photography would become an important part of Victorian mourning rituals in the form of postmortem photos. In part, this was because photographs were quite expensive and required sitting stationary for several minutes, something that was particularly difficult for children. The stillness of death, however, offered an opportunity for the family to preserve one last memory of their beloved child, who was often posed as if they were sleeping, surrounded by stuffed animals or flowers, or in the arms of a parent.

Importantly, these photos wouldn't have been considered disturbing or uncomfortable. It was a small way of keeping the dead alive, as we have been doing for thousands of years.

These advances in mainstream science and increasing secularization during the Victorian era also caused some to turn their eyes toward uncovering the secrets of the afterlife outside of the explanations offered by traditional religious dogma.

In 1848, news spread of two sisters who claimed to be communicating with a ghost in their small home in Hydesville, New York, United States. The sisters, Maggie and Kate Fox (more commonly referred to jointly as the Fox sisters), suddenly became the faces of a new religious movement known as Spiritualism that grew to have millions of believers in the years that followed. The girls "talked" to their ghost (named Charles) by asking questions and waiting for his responses in the form of knocks and raps, and they said he reached out to them from beyond the grave to let the living know that there was life after death.

All of a sudden, ghosts were no longer fearsome creatures for the Victorians, but potentially beloved family members or friends they could communicate with. The Fox sisters, now recognized across the United States and Europe as mediums for their ability to communicate with the dead, began holding public séances. Other self-proclaimed mediums quickly sprang up around the world, also offering their talents to those interested in contacting the other side.

The Rise of Modern Skepticism

For many Victorians, Spiritualism and séances were a seemingly scientific way to prove the existence of an afterlife at a time when many felt their faith was faltering or being challenged. But Spiritualism was not without its critics. For example, the Society for Psychical Research (SPR) — which still exists today! — was established in 1882 in the United Kingdom with the goal of conducting more rigorous investigations of paranormal phenomena.

Members of the group quickly got to work exposing the tricks used by fraudulent mediums by hosting their own public, fake séances. Then, in 1888, Maggie Fox gave an interview in the *New York World* claiming she and her sister perpetrated a hoax and employed simple tricks like bumping an apple along the ground using a string and cracking their toe joints to create the mysterious knocks and raps heard in their childhood home and their séances. She would later recant her confession, but the damage to the Spiritualist movement was done, and those who still believed rejected her.

Ghosts Today

The rest, as they say, is history, but the allure of a ghostly afterlife still haunts us today. Since 2014, Chapman University has conducted the Survey of American Fears, aimed at quantifying and tracking trends in the top fears of people living in the United States. The results of the 2016–2018 surveys showed a year-over-year increase of the belief that "places can be haunted by spirits," rising from 46.6 percent to 56.9 percent.

Statistics aside, all it really takes to verify our strong and growing interest in ghosts and so-called haunted places is a simple internet search. Type in "ghosts" and you'll be presented with dozens of documentaries, reality shows, and fictional movies and TV shows all focused on capturing evidence of—or scaring the pants off you with—stories about hauntings.

Countless books have been written on the subject and a never-ending supply of blurry photographs and videos on social media of so-called ghost encounters is readily available. With this ongoing fascination in mind, we could say that ghosts are an inherent part of the human experience, but does that mean they are real?

THE SCIENCE OF GHOST ENCOUNTERS

Reader, it is at this point that I must ask you to do the unthinkable and put down this book, but only for a few minutes to send a text to a few friends and family members asking them if they've ever seen a ghost. What I am sure you will find, as I often have, is that a not-insignificant number of people in your familial or social circles will have some unexplained experience to tell you about that they attributed to a ghost.

We can even back that up with data: A 2021 YouGov survey revealed that a whopping 20 percent of respondents claimed they had "seen or been in [the] presence of a ghost." If we extrapolate these numbers to the entire adult population of the United States, which was approximately 260 million people according to the 2020 Census, we can estimate that up to 52 million people in the United States alone have seen, heard, or otherwise interacted with what they believe was a ghost.

Yet with all these purported sightings or interactions, and at least 5,000 years of documented stories, there currently exists no irrefutable scientific evidence of the existence of ghosts. What do exist are many scientific explanations for ghost encounters that pertain to medical, psychological, or environmental factors that could affect or, in many cases, have affected those who've encountered "ghosts." In this section, we'll explore some of the most common and compelling of those explanations.

DOTH MY BRAIN DECEIVE ME?

Setting aside hoaxes, if we want to find logical explanations for ghost encounters, the best place to start is often the human brain, which, as it turns out, is a very weird place. A common phrase uttered on the podcast is "brains are weird," and Paige and I frequently find ourselves vastly more creeped out by the tricks our own brains can play on us compared to anything paranormal we discuss. When it comes to ghosts, it's cliché, but it might actually be all in our heads.

According to emeritus professor Chris French of the Anomalistic Psychology Research Unit at Goldsmiths College, University of London, the two most important psychological factors involved in having a so-called ghost encounter are a belief in ghosts and preexisting knowledge that a location is considered haunted. And I'll be honest, that statement alone—and the fact that there are a multitude of psychological studies backing it up—almost makes the rest of this section seem superfluous. At a minimum, it calls into question any experiences people report at well-known "haunted" locations, and with the influence of social media spreading those stories far and wide, it's perhaps not so surprising anymore that belief in ghosts and supposed ghost sightings are as common as they are.

BELIEVING IS SEEING

We'll address the belief factor first. Simply put, if you believe in ghosts, you will be more likely to interpret things that many would say are inherent to almost any creepy, old, or abandoned building, such as strange noises, unusual smells, or feelings of unease, as evidence that a given location is haunted.

A psychological study by Dr. Richard Wiseman and several colleagues published in the *Journal of Parapsychology* demonstrated this very thing. Wiseman and his research associates compared the experiences of over four hundred believers and disbelievers after they walked around a reportedly haunted area of Hampton Court Palace. This over-five-hundred-year-old castle is purportedly one of the most haunted places in England and is said to be home to many ghosts, but the most famous are likely its first ones. A few years after its construction in the early 1500s, Hampton Court was gifted to Henry VIII, and two of his six wives may have never left. Jane Seymour, Henry's third wife, died in childbirth, and it's claimed she reappears as a lady in white on the anniversary of her death. Henry's fifth wife, Catherine Howard, was executed for adultery at the Tower of London, but visitors reportedly hear her lingering screams from when guards dragged her back through one of the galleries in Hampton Court after an attempt to run to her husband and plead for her life.

It was to this very gallery, known as the Haunted Gallery, or another "haunted" space called the Georgian Rooms, that Wiseman and his colleagues chose to send their brave study participants. Volunteers were asked to wander about the spaces and note any strange occurrences, as well as mark their location on provided floor plans. The 462 participants noted a total of 431 unusual experiences between the two rooms, the majority of which were temperature changes. Additional experiences included various unusual physical feelings (such as sudden headaches and dizziness), a sense of a force or presence, bad smells, and strong emotional responses. Afterward, they were asked to rate how likely they felt that these experiences were due to an encounter with a ghost. Upon analyzing the questionnaires and maps, Wiseman and his team found that believers were not only significantly more likely to report having unusual experiences relative to disbelievers, but they were also more likely to attribute those experiences to ghosts.

Cognitive Considerations

◆─◆─◆

The exact reason why believers are more likely to experience ghosts isn't known, but it may come down to fundamental differences in the cognitive styles of believers relative to skeptics, or nonbelievers. Before you panic or get too excited, cognitive style is not a reflection of intelligence but is rather the way our brains process and interpret information. Research suggests that believers tend to employ a more intuitive style of thinking, whereas skeptics are more often analytical thinkers.

In layman's terms, this simply means that believers have a "trust-their-gut" mentality when it comes to solving problems and rely more on their feelings and intuition. Nonbelievers, on the other hand, are slower to reach their conclusions and require facts and evidence to back them up. Believers may also be more susceptible to confirmation bias, meaning they tend to only take into account evidence that backs up their already established beliefs and will attribute a deeper meaning to random coincidences.

Or Maybe the Answer is Ghosts

The maps from the Haunted Gallery in the experiment discussed on page 34 held an additional spooky surprise for Wiseman and his colleagues. The participants in the experiment had no prior knowledge of the specific locations of ghost stories associated with the Gallery. Despite this, the locations that volunteers marked on their maps as places where they had unusual experiences matched up with historical records of where others reported ghost activity in the gallery.

Wiseman, of course, believes there is still some psychological or environmental factor at play. He speculated that perhaps these were the darker and inherently creepier portions of the gallery, or, given that most of the experiences reported were temperature related, there may have been a correlation with drafts from the many concealed doors present around the space.

There is, however unlikely it may be, a possibility that this coincidence means the gallery is actually haunted. I argue that it makes for some of the most compelling evidence that ghosts could exist, given that the data was collected and analyzed in a scientifically valid manner. It definitely puts Hampton Court Palace near the top of my "Haunted" Places Bucket List, although I probably know too much about it to be a reliable witness now.

CAN I MAKE A SUGGESTION?

◆◆◆

Studies have also been conducted on the power of suggestion and its influence on the likelihood that people report ghost encounters. Imagine you're called over to babysit at a friend's house. You arrive, and after you get the normal briefing on dinner and bedtime routines, your friend mentions they've been experiencing weird things in the house, leading them to conclude that they have a resident ghost.

Now, picture yourself sitting alone in that house after the kids have gone to sleep—you'd probably expect to feel a bit on edge, right? And, if you're like me, you'd also be furiously texting your best friend (hi, Paige!) minute-by-minute updates of every paranoid thought you have about any and all strange sounds or other phenomena you think you've experienced. Well, more than just making you feel a bit uneasy for the evening, your (possibly now ex-) friend made it more likely that you will actually see, or otherwise encounter, a ghost. Or at least your brain will think you have. This is known as psychological priming.

The connection between psychological priming and ghost encounters was demonstrated in a parapsychology study from 1997 conducted by Rense Lange and James Houran at the University of Illinois at Springfield. For this study, twenty-two volunteers were sent into a theater that had no prior reputation for being haunted. Half of the volunteers were warned about recent ghost activity in the building and the other half were just told it was under renovation. A stark difference was observed between the two groups.

Those in the "haunted theater" group experienced significantly more strange occurrences and sensations compared to the "renovation" group. Forgoing the unlikely possibility that this location was actually haunted, it follows that the simple power of suggestion was enough to create ghosts in the minds of the participants. And as in our babysitting example, where it's easy to imagine spending the evening jumping at any little noise or movement, hypervigilance in response to fear appears to play a significant role in fueling these false hauntings.

This was demonstrated in another Lange and Houran study examining individuals who reported poltergeist-like encounters. The results indicated that belief, experience, and fear of the paranormal were linked together in a positive-feedback loop within the minds of their subjects, with each aspect of the loop feeding upon and reinforcing the others. In simple terms, the more you believe, the more you experience, and the more likely you are to be afraid, which then makes you believe more—and on and on it goes.

The Measure of a Nonbeliever

I keep using the terms believers and nonbelievers or skeptics, but how is "belief" actually measured when it comes to ghosts or, more broadly, the paranormal? Several standardized questionnaires exist in parapsychology that attempt to categorize or quantify believers and nonbelievers. One popular example is psychologist Michael Thalbourne's Australian Sheep-Goat Scale (ASGS). The name is a reference to a Bible passage in which Christ is said to separate the sheep (believers) from the goats (nonbelievers). It asks people to rate each of a series of eighteen questions about extra-sensory perception (ESP, or psychic powers), psychokinesis (manipulating objects with the mind), and life after death (ghosts) as "false" (worth 0 points), "uncertain" (worth 1 point), or "true" (worth 2 points). The higher your score, the more belief you have in paranormal phenomena.

A PROBLEM OF PERCEPTION

In the studies discussed in the previous section, many participants, including both believers and nonbelievers, saw or otherwise perceived things that weren't there. For some, that might be cause for concern, but as it turns out, most of what we experience on a day-to-day basis isn't necessarily "real," at least based on how some might define the concept. One of the most unsettling and fascinating parts about how our bodies and brains work is that we only perceive a small portion of the world around us, and the rest is actually our brains filling in the gaps.

It follows, then, that if our brains are constantly working to provide us with their best interpretation of visual and other stimuli in our environment, sometimes things can get a little mixed up. And when they get mixed up, we might see, hear, or feel things that aren't there, meaning that we hallucinate. Despite the stigma that having hallucinations means a person is mentally unwell, they are actually remarkably common and, in the vast majority of cases, completely benign. Even something as simple and common as feeling phantom vibrations from your phone in your pocket when you haven't gotten any notifications is considered a mild hallucination. In the context of a potentially haunted location, it's easy to see how small, commonplace tricks of the mind could become a "ghost."

APOPHENIA AND PAREIDOLIA

A major factor in the brain's ability to invent ghost encounters out of thin air is its love of patterns. As I mentioned above, the human brain is immensely powerful when it comes to filtering and processing the constant stream of visual and other stimuli being fed to us from our environment, but in its quest to determine what's important, that same powerful brain can sometimes struggle with ambiguity as it tries to make sense of our surroundings.

When faced with ambiguous input, the brain may start to see connections between unrelated things or assign meaning to random coincidences, a phenomenon known as apophenia. At some point in human evolution, apophenia may have been beneficial for survival—better to assume that rustling in the bushes is a hungry bear and head back to safety rather than find out the hard way it wasn't *just* a rabbit. If we're thinking about ghosts, ambiguous stimuli might come in the form of a lack of visual stimuli in a dark room, an odd smudge in an antique mirror, or indiscernible noises caught on a recording device. Because we are social creatures, our brains have an affinity for all things human: like calls to like. So, the dark room is suddenly populated by a shadow figure rather than a pile of laundry, the mirror has a ghostly face in it, and the random noise becomes a voice from the beyond.

Visual apophenia is known more commonly as pareidolia. This is the phenomena responsible for people seeing Jesus's face on their toast, the shapes of animals in the clouds, or the famous man on the moon. The same areas of the brain involved in facial recognition activate when face pareidolia occurs, and our inclination to see human faces in inanimate objects is again an evolutionary throwback. Those who were better at recognizing familiar, friendly faces likely had better chances of survival.

In relation to the paranormal, studies show that differences exist between believers and skeptics regarding their susceptibility to pareidolia, and more broadly, apophenia. In one such study by Tapani Riekki at the University of Helsinki, participants were shown animated videos of shapes moving randomly around the screen. Believers in the paranormal were more likely to attribute meaning to their movements. For example, they felt that certain shapes were playing tag with one another.

Another similar study by Michiel van Elk from the University of Amsterdam found that paranormal believers were more likely to see human shapes among random light displays. Believers are also more likely to see faces in distorted or otherwise ambiguous photographs and more generally, will find patterns and meaning when presented with ambiguous information relative to skeptics. Kudos, believers, on having the evolutionary advantage!

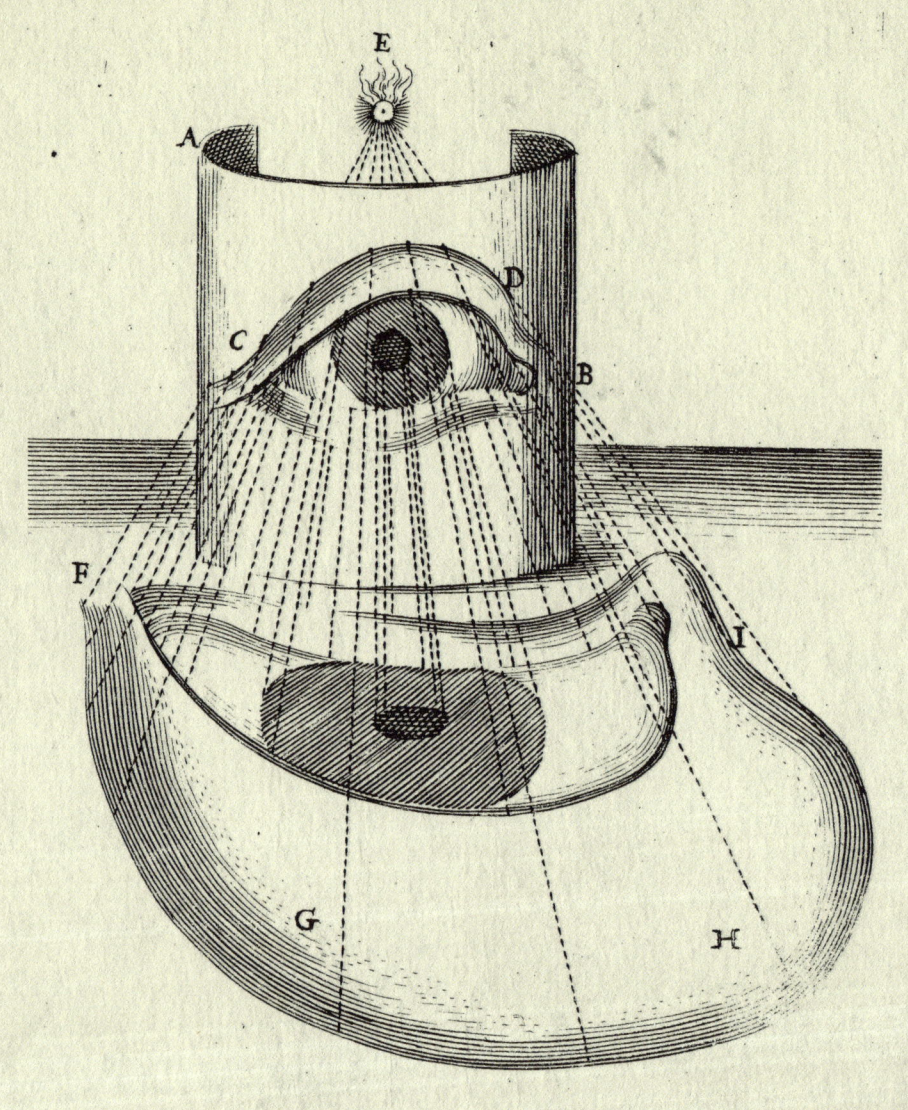

Did Anyone See That Dancing Gorilla?

At the same time that our brains can fill in the gaps in our perception with things that are not there, they can also cause us to miss significant details in our surroundings, especially if we are focused on something else. In psychology, this is referred to as inattentional blindness, and with respect to ghosts, it means that we can easily miss details that could help us find a rational explanation for a suspected encounter.

One of the most famous demonstrations of inattentional blindness was a study conducted by Daniel Simons and Christopher Chabris at Harvard University. They asked participants to watch a video of two teams of people passing basketballs. Each team consisted of three people, and participants watching the video were instructed to keep count of the number of times the ball was passed between members of one of the teams. A little over halfway through the video, a woman either carrying an open umbrella or wearing a gorilla suit walks through the middle of the activity over a period of about five seconds.

This seems like it would be difficult to miss, but remarkably, almost 50 percent of the participants did not report seeing anything unusual when they were surveyed after the fact. Notably, failing to notice something because the observer is focused elsewhere could easily explain "ghost" activity, like objects that mysteriously materialize in new locations or disembodied voices that are captured on recordings when they "*swear* no one else was around!"

In real-world scenarios, many factors can contribute to our struggle to recall details of events (or notice them at all), and unsurprisingly, they are essentially all on display in any popular ghost-hunting reality television program you might come across. These factors include poor viewing conditions (for example, darkness), fast-moving or only briefly visible stimuli, being sleepy or otherwise impaired (all-nighter in a "haunted" house, anyone?), and heightened emotions (for example, excitement, anger, or fear). Basically, although people want to believe that seeing something (or not seeing it) with their own eyes is reliable evidence that what they experienced was real, studies show time and again that our brains have quite the knack for making things up or missing them entirely.

THE DOCTOR WILL SEE YOU NOW: MENTAL HEALTH CONSIDERATIONS

Although hallucinations are common and often do not indicate any problem with a person's brain, they can be a sign that all is not well. As you might expect, schizophrenia is the go-to suggestion when it comes to seeing or hearing things that are not there. Auditory and visual hallucinations are an early sign of the onset of the disease, which affects about 1 percent of the world's population. These hallucinations have certainly been the source of some ghost encounters throughout history, especially in times before the existence of mental health conditions was recognized or as accepted as it is today. Other psychiatric conditions associated with hallucinations include bipolar disorder and post-traumatic stress disorder.

Neurologic Disorders

Beyond psychiatric disorders, there are several diseases associated with neurological symptoms that could very well be mistaken for ghosts. For example, some forms of epilepsy can elicit visions of a threatening shadow person during seizures. This was discovered by accident by neurologists during a session with an epileptic patient in which they were stimulating different parts of her brain using electrical pulses to try to determine the source of her seizures. When they activated a region of the brain called the temporoparietal junction (TPJ), the patient shocked her doctors when she reported that she sensed a shadow person close behind her, mimicking the position and movements of her body. They then asked her to read a card she held in her right hand, and the patient responded that the "man" tried to take the card from her and didn't want her to read it.

Neurologists think this occurred because the TPJ is involved in the brain's perception of the body within the environment, or our sense of "self." If this is disrupted, as it can be during seizures, our brains might perceive two bodies instead of one, and mistake the double for a ghostly being hovering a bit too close for comfort. And the TPJ isn't alone as a potential source of ghosts. Another portion of the brain, the right temporal lobe, is a possible cause of alleged poltergeist activity, as patients with damage to that portion of their brain sometimes report that they see objects move on their own, among other illusory phenomena.

Hallucinations are also incredibly common in patients with Parkinson's disease, a neurodegenerative disease that most people associate only with physical symptoms like tremors and difficulty moving. It's estimated that about half of Parkinson's patients experience some type of hallucinations. They can be simple, nonthreatening sensations of presence, or in some cases, vivid, terrifying visual hallucinations of ghosts or monsters. Parkinson's disease is also the second most common neurodegenerative disease next to Alzheimer's, making it another clear candidate for some portion of reported ghost sightings.

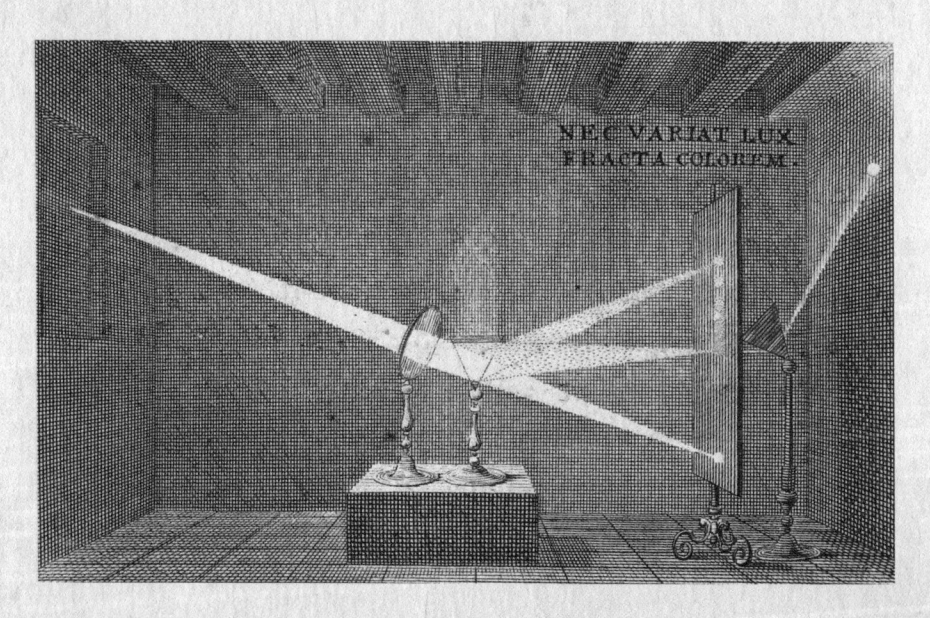

Sleep Paralysis

◆◆◆

One of the most common disorders associated with ghost encounters is a type of parasomnia, or abnormal sleep behavior, known as sleep paralysis. Sleep paralysis occurs when the brain becomes conscious while in the rapid eye movement (REM) stage of sleep, during which the muscles are paralyzed. We experience dreams during REM sleep, so this paralysis is actually a safety measure to prevent us from accidentally hurting ourselves by attempting to act out our dreams.

However, waking up unable to move, make a sound, or even breathe deeply is obviously a frightening and sometimes panic-inducing experience for most people. It is also a remarkably common one, with an estimated 8 to 20 percent of people experiencing sleep paralysis at least once. Of those who do, about 5 percent experience vivid hallucinations such as apparitions of people or monsters, hearing voices, the sensation of being held down, and intense feelings of dread.

Sleep paralysis as a logical explanation for ghost activity is especially relevant when it comes to full-bodied apparitions. Analysis of data collected on the nature and context of ghost experiences by James Houran found that only 1 percent of encounters are of the full-bodied type, and of that subset, most are seen at the foot of people's beds when they are on the verge of sleep or have just woken up.

IT'S ENVIRONMENTAL, MY DEAR WATSON!

We've established that the human brain is perfectly capable of inventing ghosts all on its own, but sometimes it gets a helping hand from something in our environment. There are several common substances that are known to induce hallucinations or cause other strange symptoms that could be mistaken for paranormal activity.

Silent but Deadly: Carbon Monoxide

Carbon monoxide (CO) is a colorless, odorless gas that is produced by gas appliances, such as fireplaces and furnaces. Symptoms of exposure include, but are not limited to, dizziness, confusion, and hallucinations. Poorly vented fireplaces, gas lamps, and a lack of modern building codes likely resulted in a large number of "ghost" encounters in the past, although it can still be an issue today. In a famous recent example, journalist and podcaster Carrie Poppy began hearing voices, feeling pain and pressure in her chest, and an overwhelming sense of dread while living in a small guesthouse. She feared she was being terrorized by some ghost or demon, and during a desperate Google search, stumbled onto a forum of paranormal skeptics who advised her to test for carbon monoxide. She immediately called the gas company, who was able to confirm the presence of a gas leak as the source of her "haunting."

Moldy Oldies

◆━━◆━━◆

Another environmental culprit thought to be a source of suspected ghost encounters is toxic mold. Breathing in spores from certain varieties of fungus can have significant neurological effects, including anxiety, depression, disorientation, memory problems, and hallucinations.

A possible link between hauntings and mold was found by Shane Rogers of Clarkson University, who was inspired to look into the issue after a mold problem in his own home caused his children to exhibit strange behavior. It occurred to Rogers that most purportedly haunted locations are in older buildings, many of which lack proper ventilation and are thus more likely to have mold issues. He, along with a team of students, conducted air sampling tests to determine the prevalence of mold spores in twenty-three buildings, some of which were reported to be haunted and some that were not. Although the results have yet to be published (and thus be subjected to the all-important peer review), Rogers reported that they found up to five to six times the amount of mold spores in the "haunted" buildings as in the nonhaunted ones.

Pick Your Poison

◆◆◆

There exists a wide variety of additional substances that, if ingested or otherwise introduced to the body, can cause serious neurological impairment. Sometimes, of course, people purposefully ingest substances that might make them see or otherwise encounter things that aren't there. For example, people have reported spiritual or ghostlike encounters while under the influence of certain psychedelic drugs. Other times, people are exposed accidentally and/or aren't aware of the possible side effects of some toxic substance. This was especially true before modern food, drug, and industrial safety regulations.

Check the ingredients on some so-called health tonics from the Victorian era and you might find yourself more surprised that anyone managed to *not* see (or, for that matter, become) ghosts during that time. Mercury, also known as quicksilver, was an ingredient in medicines for hundreds of years up until the 1950s. Calomel, a type of mercury-based salt (Hg_2Cl_2), was commonly prescribed for a wide variety of illnesses. Parents were even instructed to rub the powder on babies' gums to relieve teething pain. In 1921, the mother of a child suffering from mercury poisoning because of this practice said, "If she was an adult, she would have been considered to be insane, sitting up in her cot, banging her head with her hands, tearing out her hair, screaming, and viciously scratching anyone who came near."

Combined with neurological symptoms reported in adults such as visual disturbances and behavioral changes, these behaviors could certainly be mistaken for a person being tormented by some invisible, supernatural force. Similarly, lead exposure can cause drastic shifts in behavior, as well as anxiety, delirium, hallucinations, and memory loss.

Did You Hear That?

Outside of exposure to toxic substances, some have postulated that ghost encounters may be the result of reactions to environmental phenomena like infrasound or strong electromagnetic fields (EMF). The idea that infrasound could cause a haunting was pioneered in the late 1990s by an engineer named Vic Tandy, who sought to explain his own personal ghost encounter. Tandy was working late one night when feelings of dread and the sense of a presence in the room overwhelmed him. Out of the corner of his eye, he saw a ghostly figure, but when he turned to face it, the figure disappeared. Tandy had heard the facility was supposedly haunted but remained skeptical and started searching for a cause. What he found was a recently installed fan humming at a frequency of 18.9 hertz (Hz), just below the threshold of 20 Hz detectable by human ears, meaning that the fan was producing infrasound.

Turns out, although it is imperceptible to us, our eyeballs vibrate at a similar frequency (gross, right?). Tandy therefore proposed that the addition of infrasound created a disruption in his peripheral vision and induced vibrations in other internal organs that caused his false sense of panic, a hypothesis that he backed up with a study published in 2000 that measured infrasound in a "haunted" fourteenth-century cellar in Coventry, England.

It is worth noting that some have criticized Tandy's methods from that study, and a subsequent investigation of the same cellar by Steve Parsons, a cofounder of the independent research group Para.Science, found low levels of a broad range of low-frequency sound waves with no particular concentration around 19 Hz. That said, this and other studies by Parsons showed that high levels of infrasound, just not necessarily focused at 19 Hz, are associated with reports of ghostly activity. In a "haunted" location, sources of infrasound could include wind blowing across an open window or chimney, the distant rumbling of traffic, machinery, geologic or geomagnetic activity, and many other natural or man-made phenomena.

DÉJÀ BOO

A ghost story, written by William Wilmer and published in the 1921 medical journal *The American Journal of Ophthalmology*, chronicles Mrs. H and her family's experience living in a haunted house. Shortly after moving into their new home Mrs. H and her husband began experiencing the classic signs of a Hollywood house haunting. The whole household heard unknown voices, footsteps, and the thumps of moving furniture. Things took a turn for the worse when they fell ill and began suffering from headaches, moments of paralysis, and apparition sightings.

Like many of us would, Mr. and Mrs. H considered abandoning their new home. But when the family was visited by Mr. H's brother, they learned the house might not be haunted after all. He believed, after reading another family's story, that Mr. and Mrs. H were experiencing symptoms of carbon monoxide poisoning. To the family's surprise, he was right. They weren't living in a haunted house; they were living in a house with an old, faulty furnace that had been sending carbon monoxide fumes into the home. It took a doctor's visit and a repair of their furnace for their "haunting" to come to an end.

Electromagnetic Fantasies

⸺◆⸺

Electromagnetic fields (EMFs) are arguably the most well-known and supposedly scientific environmental factor when it comes to ghosts. A common tool used by paranormal investigators is an EMF meter under the guise that ghosts are capable of manipulating or even generating EMFs, a possibility that we'll discuss more in the next section.

In very simple terms, EMF refers to the complementary, or coupled, electric and magnetic fields associated with the flow of charged particles (for example, when an electric current made up of electrons flows through a wire to power a household appliance that is switched on). In the context of ghosts, research has been focused on the possibility that static or extremely low frequency (abbreviated as ELF, meaning low energy) EMFs may, much like infrasound, stimulate the temporal lobe and cause hallucinations. Sources of ELF-EMFs are everywhere in today's world. Every electrical device you own (when turned on), including the wiring in your walls, LED light bulbs, and the power lines outside your house, emits ELF-EMFs.

Research, driven mainly by the late neuropsychologist Michael Persinger, has shown that ELF-EMFs can affect the temporal lobe in particularly sensitive individuals, causing them to hallucinate. Some studies have been able to replicate Persinger's results in laboratory and real-world settings using stronger or complex ELF-EMF signals, but others have failed to do so and/or are critical of Persinger's methodology. Also, while anomalies in the strength and pattern of EMFs in certain locations can exist due to variability in natural or artificial sources, this doesn't seem to be the case for many haunted locations. Long story short, while the idea of EMF-induced hallucinations is compelling and worthy of further study, it is likely not the scientific silver bullet many believe it to be to explain ghost encounters.

Something Spooky

I've actually experienced mild hallucinations in the past, although I wouldn't have categorized them as such at the time. For example, in college, I traveled to Antarctica as a field assistant. The entire time I was there, I remember repeatedly thinking I was seeing small animals or birds moving among the rocks, especially out of the corner of my eye. Of course, there are no such creatures on that continent, and any animal life that was present at the time was out at the coast or the edge of the ice shelf, over sixty miles (96 km) away from where I was located.

I've also experienced these types of visual hallucinations after the loss of a pet. For weeks afterward, I'll find myself thinking I've just seen them dart around a corner or into an empty room. In both examples, my brain was accustomed to having those things around, so it decided to add a little spice back into its interpretation of my surroundings, and I got to spend a few weeks seeing things that weren't there.

Test Your Knowledge

Haunted Houses

Haunted or not? Guess what famously "haunted" United States location is referenced in each of the facts/stories below.

▲

A. Construction on this twenty-four thousand square foot (2,230 m²) home began in the late 1800s and took over three decades to complete. The story goes that the 24/7 construction and unique features, including unusually short staircases leading into walls or ceilings and windows looking into other rooms of the home, were used to evade and confuse vengeful spirits. In late 1924, Harry Houdini visited this location on his tour to debunk Spiritualism (there was even a Houdini-themed escape room on-site for a short time).

◻

B. This hotel, located in Colorado and built in 1909, is considered one of the most haunted places in the United States. It is famously known for being Stephen King's inspiration for the Overlook Hotel in his book *The Shining* after King claimed to have had a particularly frightening stay involving ghostly sightings and unusual lucid dreams. Since the publication of *The Shining*, the hotel has embraced its "haunted" reputation and offers a number of different evening and paranormal tours.

Answers on page 200

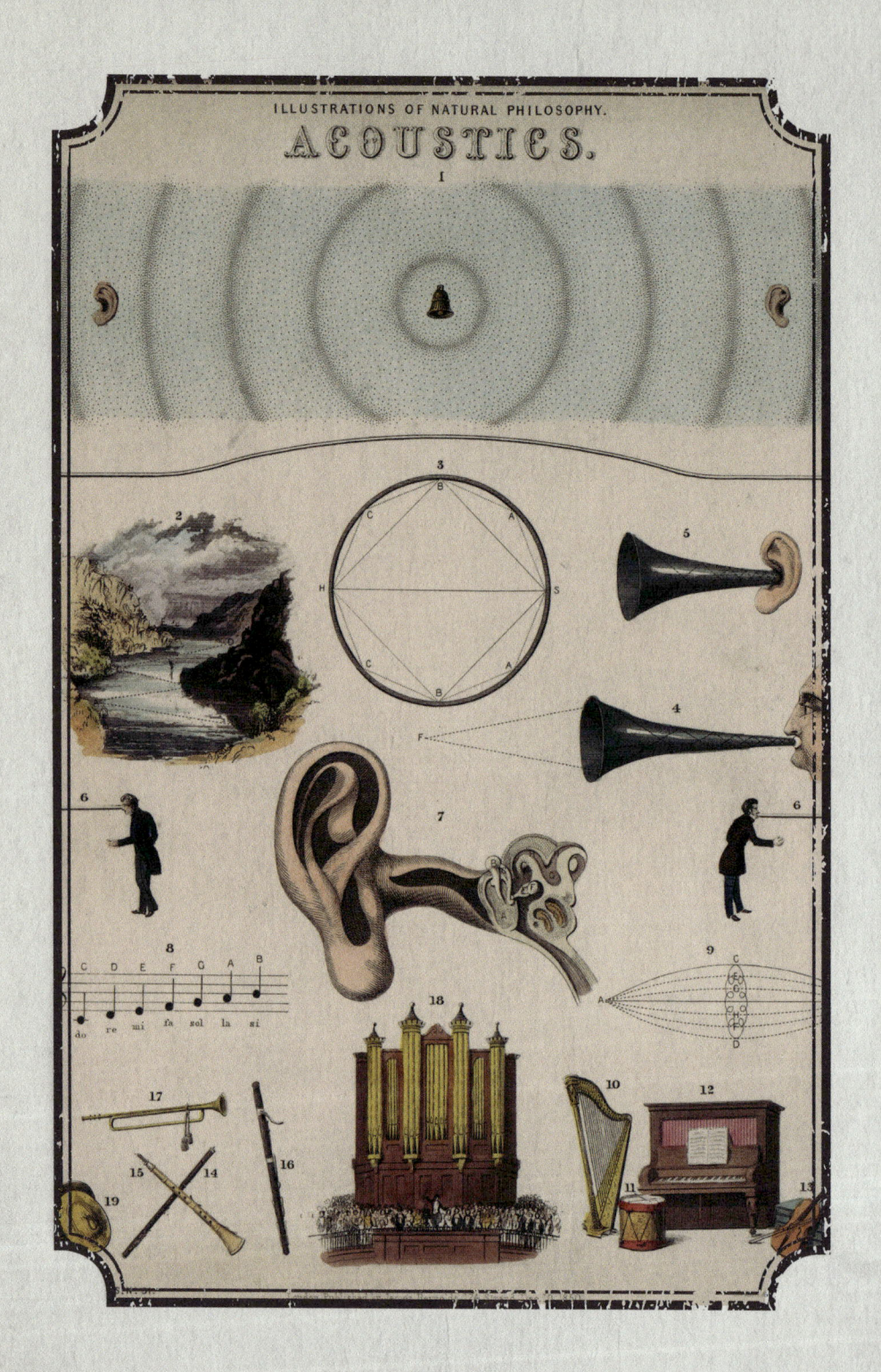

ILLUSTRATIONS OF NATURAL PHILOSOPHY.
ACOUSTICS.

THE "SCIENCE" OF PARANORMAL INVESTIGATION

In the previous section, we established that the human brain is easily fooled into believing it has encountered a ghost. Given this, perhaps what is needed is a nonhuman tool to observe and document ghostly phenomena. While it is our belief that mainstream science and logic can explain most (or probably all) ghostly encounters, that hasn't stopped the development of a large and lucrative industry aimed at capturing evidence of the paranormal. Emphasis on the word "lucrative" (and bonus points if it looks good on TV). So, let's consider the scientific validity of some of the tools commonly employed by paranormal investigators. Fair warning, it's about to get a little snarky.

SAY CHEESE!: GHOSTS ON CAMERA

Given that ghosts are noncorporeal and we can't count on capturing tangible evidence, obtaining photographic or video evidence of them is of paramount importance to any effort to prove their existence. Go on any public ghost tour and you can pretty much guarantee the guide will tell you to have your camera ready and to keep snapping photos throughout the tour because you might just catch something that wasn't visible to the naked eye.

In addition to priming you to have a paranormal experience during the tour, the guide is also using the power of suggestion to ensure that you interpret any ambiguous smudge or shadow in your photos as evidence of a ghost. The presence of these types of features is made only more likely by the fact that most ghost tours take place at night, when even the best cell phone cameras will start to struggle. That said, even with access to professional-grade camera equipment, paranormal investigators and television shows still fail to capture anything conclusive when it comes to photos or videos of ghosts. In most, if not all, cases photographic or video evidence of ghosts is the result of one or more of the following nonparanormal phenomena:

PAREIDOLIA

If you're taking photos or videos to look for ghosts, chances are your brain will find one for you, especially if the photos are taken under low-light conditions. There are countless photos uploaded to social media with the insistence that there is a face or human shape hidden among a shadowy portion of the image. This also applies to blurred, distorted "apparitions" captured in tarnished mirrors or through old windows with wavy, hand-blown panes.

Ask any skeptic, myself included, and they'll tell you most images or videos of ghosts—and this includes the ones captured by so-called professional paranormal investigators—can be chalked up to pareidolia and wishful thinking. It's also common for people to enhance the images by turning up the contrast and brightness or adding something like a circle or arrow to highlight the area of interest, increasing the chances that people will see something, simply because they've been told they should or because of distortion created by overprocessing.

VISUAL ARTIFACTS

Once digital cameras and handheld video cameras became available, a new type of ghostly image began to appear: the orb. Believers (or at least ghost-hunting television personalities) suggest that orbs, which typically look like white, transparent circles or halos in photos or videos, are ghosts or some other spiritual beings manifesting as balls of energy.

In all likelihood, they are reflections of light off out-of-focus things that are close to the camera lens, like bugs, dust, water droplets, or a lens flare from a nearby light source or the camera's own flash reflecting off of the lens. Anomalies that are not round could be as simple as out-of-focus strands of hair or camera straps. All these things became more likely given the smaller focal length of more compact, digital, and cell phone cameras with built-in flashes. Orbs can also appear in video footage, including when they are in night mode, for the same reasons.

Orbs are so common, in fact, that many home security companies address them in the frequently asked questions pages on their websites, reassuring customers that they are not a sign of anything paranormal afoot.

HOAXES AND ILLUSIONS

There's always the chance that a ghost in an image is the result of fakery. At the height of the Spiritualism movement (see page 29), "spirit photographs" were immensely popular and were created via double exposures. The extra person (the "ghost") in the image appeared transparent and indistinct because they were either a remnant of another portrait left on a recycled glass plate or were added by only momentarily opening the shutter to expose the plate a second time. (Recall that photo exposures required tens of seconds—up to several minutes—with early cameras.) Later, it was also possible to create double exposures using modern film cameras.

Another popular way to create a "ghost" during the Victorian era was using an illusion called Pepper's Ghost, named for a traveling scientist and lecturer named John Henry Pepper. The illusion works by reflecting the image of a hidden performer onto a pane of glass so that they suddenly appear on stage in front of an audience. If you've ever ridden the Haunted Mansion ride at Disneyland, you've experienced it! With the proper lighting and positioning of a sheet of glass or plastic, this illusion could easily be replicated to create a convincing photograph of a ghost.

Today, most ghost photos aren't captured on film cameras, so there's no chance of a double exposure, but there are plenty of applications that can manipulate photos, and they get better and better all the time. There also might just be an actual person in the photo who is disguised or obscured in some way that makes them seem supernatural, especially if the image is dark or of poor quality.

Inattentional Blindness

A feature of many ghost photo (or video) stories is that the person who took the photo didn't notice anything unusual when they captured it, and it was only when they looked at the picture or footage after the fact that they noticed a ghostly presence.

If pareidolia, a camera malfunction, or an intentional hoax can be ruled out, there's still the possibility of inattentional blindness. Someone in the photographer's group (or from outside of it) could have walked through the frame of the image without the photographer noticing at the time. Said person might appear especially ghost-like if the photographer is taking a panoramic image or using a long-exposure time. An unnoticed person could also walk behind the camera and cast a shadow or appear in a reflection within frame.

You're Getting Colder...
or Maybe Hotter?

Thermal imaging cameras detect infrared light to visualize variations in heat signatures. The most common claim is that cold spots in a room are indicative of paranormal activity because ghosts require heat energy from the surrounding environment to manifest themselves, communicate, or interact with objects. This supposedly produces cold spots, which can then be detected on thermal cameras or other temperature-sensing devices. (Also, does this mean ghost sightings should be more common in hotter places or during the summer months?)

In reality, cold spots that show up on cameras are probably nothing more than evidence of things like bad or no insulation, drafts, and air vents, combined with a dose of pareidolia to make the blue blobs seem more human shaped. Paranormal investigators also interpret hot spots on thermal images as evidence of ghost activity (I guess the ghost would be hot if it sucked the heat out of a specific spot?), but these are often easily debunked as residual heat from one of the investigation team members who has since moved or an animal.

ELECTRONIC VOICE PHENOMENA: SPIRITS IN THE STATIC?

Electronic voice phenomena (or EVP) refers to "ghostly" voices captured using sensitive audio recorders during paranormal investigations. A typical EVP session involves investigators asking questions while holding or standing around a recording device, with pauses between each inquiry to give any entities present a chance to respond. More often than not, responses from the spirit world are not heard at the time the recording is made but are noticed when reviewing the audio files after the fact.

Here's the thing, though, as someone who's spent a few hundred hours editing audio for a podcast and videos, I can attest that random, unexplained noise is just par for the course when you're recording audio in an environment that is not completely isolated from the outside world. To the credit of investigators, many tag their audio recordings by verbally acknowledging it if they make or notice an unexpected, nonparanormal noise, but they are still often missing critical controls to ensure there are no outside influences. This is especially troublesome if the so-called voices require significant amounts of amplification to amount to more than just a squiggle of noise in the audio file. How can they guarantee it wasn't someone's stomach rumbling, or there wasn't a small animal scratching around in the walls, or the HVAC system didn't kick on, or an actual person walked past the building talking on a cell phone, or, **or, or**?!

You might think these types of noises would also be noticed and tagged, but inattentional blindness could very well mean that someone who is focused on the task at hand—that is, asking questions of ghosts—wouldn't notice minor noises and goings-on around them that could contaminate the audio recording. There's also the chance of stray radio waves being picked up by microphones via radio frequency (RF) interference or cross modulation, which can manifest as a hissing noise or actual clips of songs or speech in the recording.

There are a few psychological factors behind why people might hear voices and words in random noise, including the power of suggestion, apophenia, and something called the verbal transformation effect. I, for one, am frequently a victim of the power of suggestion. When I listen to EVPs that are shared by paranormal investigators, I almost always hear nothing more than garbled sounds or random noise, even when I really try to make out a message. As soon as it's revealed what the investigators hear, though, and especially if they play the recording back with subtitles as they often do in ghost-hunting TV shows, the power of suggestion takes over and that's all I can hear. It's like when someone points out a song lyric that sounds like the singer is saying something else—from that point on, you'll always mishear it.

The investigators who interpreted the audio in the first place may have been affected by something called auditory apophenia. This has been demonstrated in a couple of experiments. One, performed by famous psychologist B.F. Skinner, found that participants heard words (with consonants) when he played them a tape of random vowel sounds. Another experiment conducted by the Society for Psychical Research asked participants to transcribe a lecture from a barely audible, poor-quality recording but then proceeded to play them a tape of nothing but white noise. Amazingly, the subjects heard and wrote down words, phrases, and even entire sentences, all thanks to apophenia enhanced by the power of suggestion. Some also think that hearing words in ambiguous audio recordings is related to the verbal transformation effect, which is a type of auditory illusion in which people begin to perceive new words when they are played the same word, or set of words, on a loop.

The Flashlight Trick

One of my favorite communication tools employed by paranormal investigators is, for lack of a better name, the flashlight trick. The flashlight trick is commonly paired with EVP sessions, as the light is seen as a secondary, visual way for the ghosts to respond to questions that are asked.

The trick requires a flashlight that turns on and off via a twisting motion of the head, which is set up so it is just barely twisted to the on or off position and then placed on a flat surface. The investigator then asks yes or no questions and requests that any spirits present turn the light on or off in response. The idea is that the ghost only has to muster enough energy for a slight touch to manipulate it.

It's a neat trick—I can remember being amazed when I first saw it on a ghost-hunting TV show—but it's not the slightest bit paranormal (womp, womp). The light is actually turning on and off by itself because of a simple heating cycle. When the bulb is on, the reflective metal cup around it expands just enough to push down on the interior components and break the circuit that powers the light—the same way the circuit is broken when you tighten down the head to turn it off. Then, as the reflector cools and contracts, the interior components shift back into place just enough to complete the circuit, and the light turns back on again. No ghosts required.

THE SPIRIT BOX: TUNING IN TO GHOSTS

Speaking of random electronic noise, another famous ghost-hunting tool is the Spirit Box (also called Frank's Box). I will be honest here—in terms of paranormal investigation equipment, I think this is one of the silliest, and least believable ones, because it's literally just noise from a broken radio! But anyway, the Spirit Box is essentially a radio that has been permanently set to scanning mode. It cycles through radio frequencies at a fast pace, and as it does, short words or snippets of words from radio broadcasts burst through the static, and listeners can string them together into full words or phrases. Just like in an EVP session, paranormal investigators ask questions, and the implication is that ghosts are somehow able to manipulate the radio waves and control the messages that emerge in response.

The benefit for investigators is that they can get immediate responses from the ghosts and not have to wait to sift through hours of audio recordings after the fact. The downside is that all they're really hearing is random bits of radio signals that their brains are trying to assemble into meaningful patterns for them under the influence of their own beliefs and biases.

One of the ways paranormal investigators try to get around the inherent biases of the Spirit Box is by employing something called the Estes Method. This is where a designated listener from the group is hooked up to the Spirit Box via noise-canceling headphones and blindfolded, so they can't hear the questions being asked or receive any visual clues from the rest of the investigators doing the asking. I will go so far as to say that this method is a step in the right direction, but the fact remains that apophenia is still an issue—the listener's brain will readily piece together words whether or not they hear the questions—and they are also not free from bias because:

- They're participating in a paranormal investigation, so they've likely been told the location is haunted and were primed with stories about the suspected ghosts.

• They've also probably been involved in previous investigations, so they are familiar with the types of questions that will be asked.

• And with or without employing the Estes Method, those interpreting the "responses" can easily fall victim to confirmation bias, meaning they pay attention only to the responses that make sense and support their belief that they are talking to an intelligent, spiritual being. Words that are heard at random times, or that don't make sense given the question asked, are ignored.

Talk Dead-y to Me

Before ghosts could talk to us via voice recorders, or by manipulating random radio signals, ghost hunters had to get their messages from the beyond the old-fashioned way: using a Ouija board (also known as a spirit board). These boards have been around since the 1890s but were popularized as a tool to contact the dead thanks to a revival of Spiritualism (page 29) that swept through the United States during World War I.

Anyone who's ever attended a sleepover where someone pulled one out probably has a spooky story about the planchette moving around the board even though everyone swore they weren't pushing it. Turns out, they might have been right! Ouija boards seem to work because of something called the ideomotor effect, which is a psychological phenomenon wherein people's own expectations and beliefs can cause them to unconsciously move their hands around the board.

It's easily demonstrated as a trick of the mind by blocking people's view of the board—their hands will still move the planchette, but they'll only produce nonsense words. Dowsing rods, another low-tech piece of equipment often pulled out for paranormal investigations, also appear to work because of the same effect.

EMF DEVICES: "GHOSTS" IN THE MACHINES

One of the common beliefs in the field of paranormal investigation is that ghosts can manifest as or manipulate electromagnetic fields. This idea is usually defended by pointing out that a fundamental law of physics and chemistry is the conservation of energy, which states that energy cannot be destroyed or created but can only change form. The suggestion is that this law means that the energy flowing between synapses in our brains, the little chemical and electrical impulses that make us *us* will persist after we die as a soul or spirit, because it's fundamentally impossible for that energy to just disappear.

It's a very nice thought that on the surface seems scientifically sound, but of course, that's not really how death works. The energy in our bodies doesn't disappear, but rather gets transferred to the billions of microbes and other organisms that immediately get to work decomposing our corpses. We don't turn into ghosts; we just get redistributed.

However, despite breaking the laws of physics, the idea that ghosts are made up of the energy left after we die is the basis for several pieces of equipment that purportedly use electromagnetic fields (EMF) to detect or communicate with the spirits of the dead. A few popular ones are:

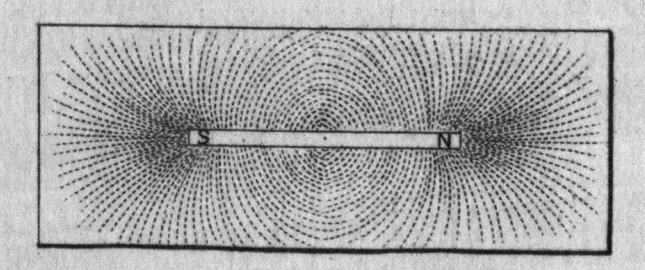

- **EMF detectors or meters:** EMF meters do exactly what their name suggests—measure electromagnetic fields—but as we learned in the previous section (see page 53), EMF is everywhere. Because it is less expensive, many ghost hunters use a single-axis meter, which requires the user to slowly rotate the device in all three dimensions to find the maximum readout. That maximum represents the total EMF present at a specific spot.

Walking around with the meter and seeing spikes is probably the result of the user moving in and out of various man-made and natural sources of EMF. Leaving the device stationary might be somewhat better, but it is still likely measuring anomalous spikes related to background EMF noise and any electronics or wiring in the room.

- **REM Pods:** The Radiating Electromagnetic Field (REM) Pod, looks like a hockey puck with some LED lights and a small antenna coming out the top. The pod generates its own EMF and can sense any disturbances within that field (which are obviously assumed to be ghosts), upon which it lights up and makes noise. Some versions also include temperature sensors.

Kenny Biddle, a Chief Investigator for the Committee for Skeptical Inquiry (or CSI), disassembled and tested a REM Pod, and found that it was simply a disguised, modified, Junior Theremin—a small, novelty version of a musical instrument. The implication is that like a person can play a theremin by moving their hands within the EMF generated by its antenna(s), the presence of a ghost in proximity will also cause it to make noise.

As with an EMF meter, contamination by other sources of electromagnetism can set off the REM Pod. Biddle's tests also found that two-way radios, which are commonly used by paranormal investigation crews, could trigger the REM Pod from twenty to forty feet (6–12 m) away. He also found he could set it off from the floors directly above and below the device.

• **Ovilus:** The Ovilus is a small, rectangular device with two antennas sticking out of the top that are used to measure EMF input, which device converts into a words from a preloaded library. Each word corresponds to a specific frequency defined by the manufacturer, and the current version, the Ovilus 5, has over two thousand words installed. It's basically a dumbed down version of a Spirit Box, in that it turns random electromagnetic frequencies into something paranormal investigators can convince themselves is meaningful.

Outside of EMF interference and investigator biases, a major issue with all these devices is that there's no clear information on exactly how or why they might work to detect ghosts. Proprietary devices like the REM Pod and Ovilus are made to look scientific, but all the data in the world means nothing if it's not collected scientifically. The manufacturers of the Ovilus even state in the disclaimers that it is meant for entertainment purposes only, that the output should not be presented as evidence of the paranormal, and they warn of the power of suggestion and that any meaningful responses are more likely to be coincidence.

Actual scientific instrumentation comes with extensive documentation about exactly what it measures and how all the components inside of it work, and all that information is backed up by many published, peer-reviewed experimental studies that demonstrate its capabilities and limitations. Any new applications, especially ones that require using the instrument in a way that is outside of what it was intended for, would be subject to fierce scrutiny by both the researchers conducting the experiments and others in the scientific community.

BooBuddy... or Foe?

If you find lurking around an old dark building searching for ghosts unnerving, maybe a talking stuffed bear will bring you comfort—or at the very least it will creep you out enough that you will forget about the otherwise terrifying situation you've put yourself in. BooBuddy is a ghost-hunting bear that incorporates several of the most popular ghost-hunting technologies (the validity of which has been discussed in the main text). Designed to respond to changes in "energy, temperature, and motion," BooBuddy is not your average, run-of-the-mill teddy bear. This ten-inch-tall (25 cm) interactive teddy is marketed as a "collaborative spirit" and the "paranormal investigator's sidekick."

So, what does it do? Once BooBuddy takes baseline measurements (EMF, temperature, positioning, etc.), it will begin reading through a series of random EVP questions to encourage a response from the supernatural. With its built-in EMF detector, BooBuddy's paws will light up when it "detects a change in EMF"; its other sensors are meant to detect a change in the environment (motion or temperature), prompting BooBuddy to react with one of its many programmed verbal responses.

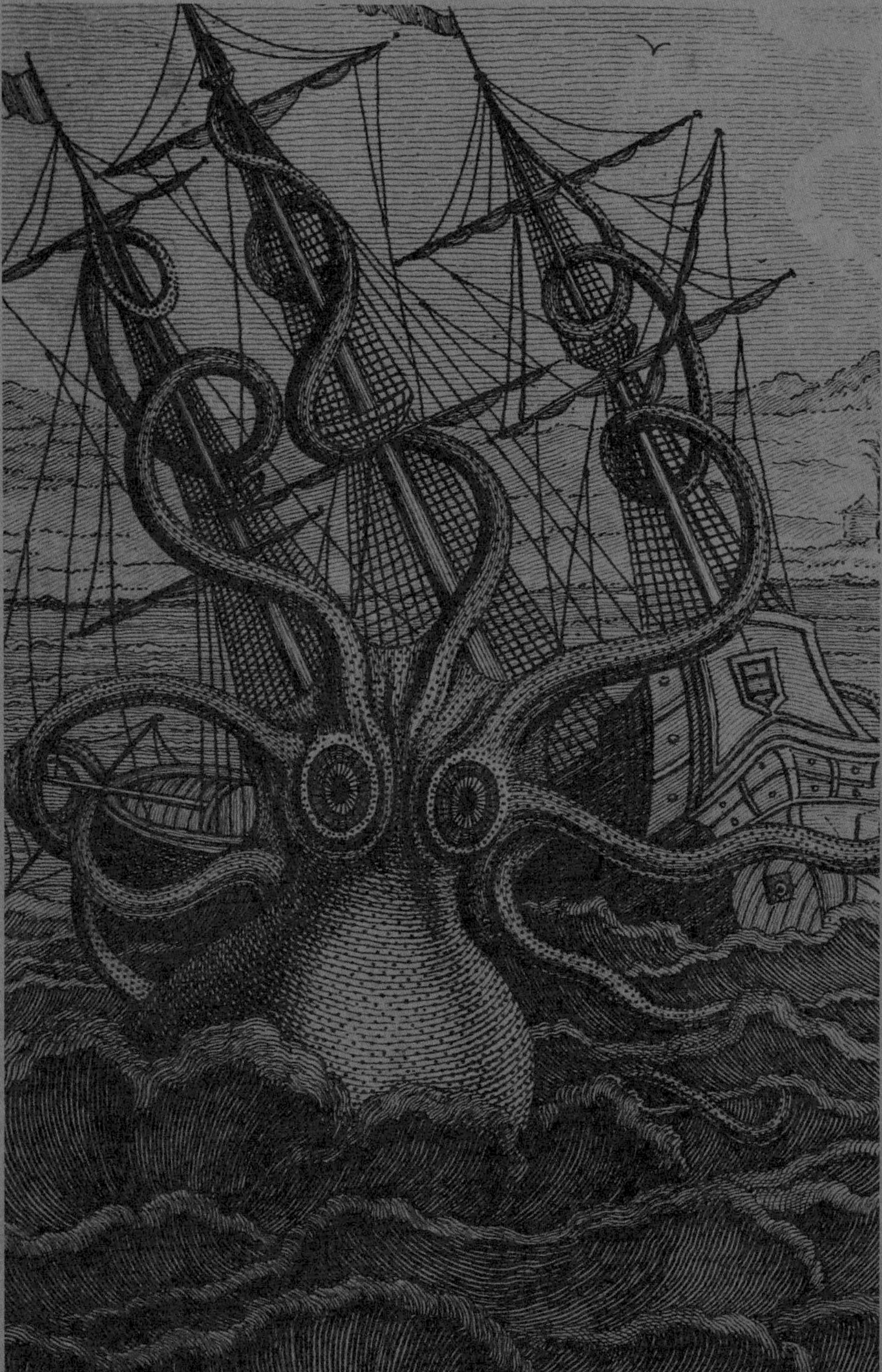

PART II
CREEPY CREATURES AND LEGENDARY FEATURES

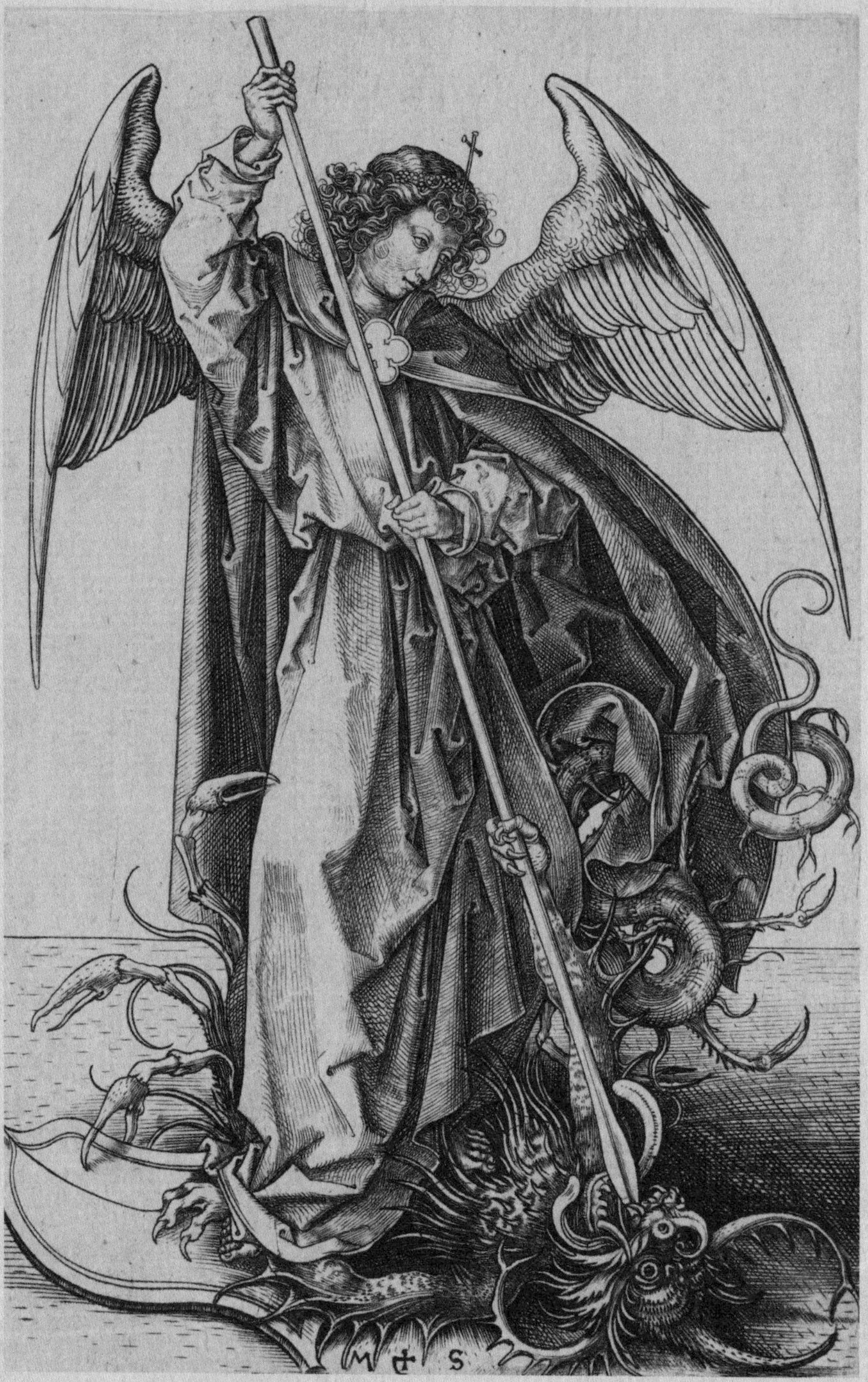
M S

MONSTERS

Humans have been telling monster stories for thousands of years, and they've served many purposes over the millennia. In some cases, they represent simple misidentifications of real animals. (Think sailors inventing the Kraken to explain giant squid sightings or dinosaur bones being mistaken for dragons; we'll talk more about this tendency in the next section on cryptids.) More often, however, they are manifestations of the collective fears of a given culture or society as well as reflections of current events.

For anxious parents, a monster story might be the perfect way to keep their adventurous child from straying too far into the woods. For medieval villagers who faced a rash of murders in their otherwise peaceful town, monsters were a convenient scapegoat to avoid confronting the monstrous deeds of their fellow man. In the wake of a pandemic or an economic or political crisis (or all three!), zombie movies and television can help to channel our fears about the collapse of society as we know it.

While monsters reside largely in the realm of fiction and metaphor today, many of them were very real to people in the past, and evidence for their existence was found in the gaps of our scientific knowledge. In this section, we'll consider three of the most popular and enduring monsters and the possible science that did (or didn't!) help to create and sustain them.

VAMPIRES

Legends of vampiric creatures exist in almost every culture and date back to ancient times. Their characteristics, including how they were transformed, how they behave or look, and ways to get rid of them can vary, but most agree that vampires must subsist on a diet of human blood or other vital fluids. They are often also considered to be a representation of our darkest desires, such as the lengths we would go to in order to escape death or our repressed sexual urges. The vampire as we know it today is primarily based on Slavic folklore and a series of peculiar events that took place in small, Serbian villages in the eighteenth century. So, let's sink our teeth into everyone's favorite bloodsuckers.

CSI: Eighteenth-Century Serbia

It was 1725, and Serbia, a country in the midst of a geopolitical struggle between the Ottoman and Habsburg Empires, had a vampire problem. That year, a man named Petar Blagojevic, who lived in the village of Kisiljevo, passed away. His death, however, reportedly wasn't as final as it should have been. About ten weeks after Blagojevic's burial, another nine people died over a period of as many days. Each of them claimed on their deathbed that Petar had paid them a visit in the night, during which he lay upon them and choked them.

So, the citizens of Kisiljevo did what any reasonable group of people would do in early eighteenth-century Serbia—they dug up his corpse to investigate and were shocked by what they found. Petar's body wasn't decaying as expected, his nails and hair had grown, and fresh blood was present around his mouth. Believing this to be evidence that he was a vampire, the villagers sprang into action and drove a stake through Petar's torso. Upon doing so, even more fresh blood spilled from his mouth and ears, so to be extra sure of his demise, they also decapitated and burned the body. The news stories from this incident marked the first time the Serbian term for these creatures, *vampyri*, appeared widely in print.

Call in the Reinforcements

Later that year, in a small village about 120 miles (193 km) away called Medvegia (also seen as Medveđa or Meduegna), another vampire emerged. Arnod Paole (often anglicized as Arnold Paul) was a soldier who had recently moved to the village from a Turkish-controlled portion of Serbia, where, among the many hardships he endured while at war, he claimed he fought and was bitten by a vampire. To avoid becoming a vampire himself, Arnod ate dirt from the vampire's tomb and rubbed its blood on the bite and the wounds it inflicted on him. Unfortunately, his time in his new home was short-lived; he passed away in an accident after just a few months, and it quickly became apparent that his attempts to avoid the vampire life (or afterlife, I guess?) were unsuccessful.

Within a few weeks, four additional people in the village dropped dead after rapid-onset, unknown illnesses, and all of them reported they were visited in the night by Arnod. And just like Petar in Kisiljevo, when the villagers dug up Arnod, his undecomposed body, the presence of fresh blood, and growth of his hair and nails told them everything they needed to know: He was a vampire. When they staked him, not only did fresh blood pour from his body, but he let out a terrifying groan, which further confirmed their suspicions. In this case, all four of Arnod's supposed victims were dug up and similarly dispatched.

For a time, it seemed like Medvegia's vampire problem was over. That is, until 1731, when at least seventeen people succumbed to a mysterious illness over a period of just a few months (I'll note that as with many paranormal stories, the numbers are a bit fuzzy depending on which source you look at). To the horror of the villagers, the symptoms of this illness were very similar to those experienced by Arnod's victims five years earlier, with one reporting that an earlier victim from the group attacked her one night when she herself became ill.

Dying to Get Out

In 1818, heavy and locked grave cages, known as mortsafes or mort-cages, were constructed and placed around gravesites in an attempt to keep out resurrectionists—body snatchers often paid by anatomists for exhumed bodies intended for use in anatomical/medical research. Cages remained in place until the decomposition progressed past the point of cadaver viability. In more recent years, videos and articles have surfaced referencing these cages as a way to keep suspected vampires in, and while that might make for a more entertaining story, the truth is the cages' purpose was to protect the deceased from the living, not the other way around.

It was time to call in reinforcements, and it wasn't long before a surgeon named Johannes Flückinger was dispatched from Vienna, Austria, to investigate. Flückinger ordered that all those recently deceased be disinterred and autopsied, and found at least thirteen who appeared unusually well-preserved, with all the tell-tale signs of vampirism and no evidence of any known disease. They were staked, beheaded, and burned, and by all accounts, Medvegia's vampire troubles finally ended.

The Birth of Modern Vampire Folklore

❖

The tale of Arnod Paole went eighteenth-century-viral, with pamphlets, treatises, and news stories sparking interest around the world in these so-called vampires. Even though the church disavowed the existence of vampires in the following decades, the cultural impact of Arnod's story was enduring and set the standards for vampire folklore as we still know it today. His and Petar Blagojevic's stories are also classic examples of what happens when folklore and science meet—even if the science was not so sound at the time—and highlight the long-standing link between the history of medical science and vampire folklore. Bram Stoker's *Dracula* leaned into this by making the main protagonist, Dr. Abraham Van Helsing, insist that medical science could explain the existence of vampires if scientists were not so close-minded (some things never change, do they?). We can even see this connection today in pop culture depictions of vampires who are doctors themselves, such as Carlisle Cullen in Stephenie Meyer's *Twilight* series or Matthew Clairmont in Deborah Harkness's All Souls trilogy.

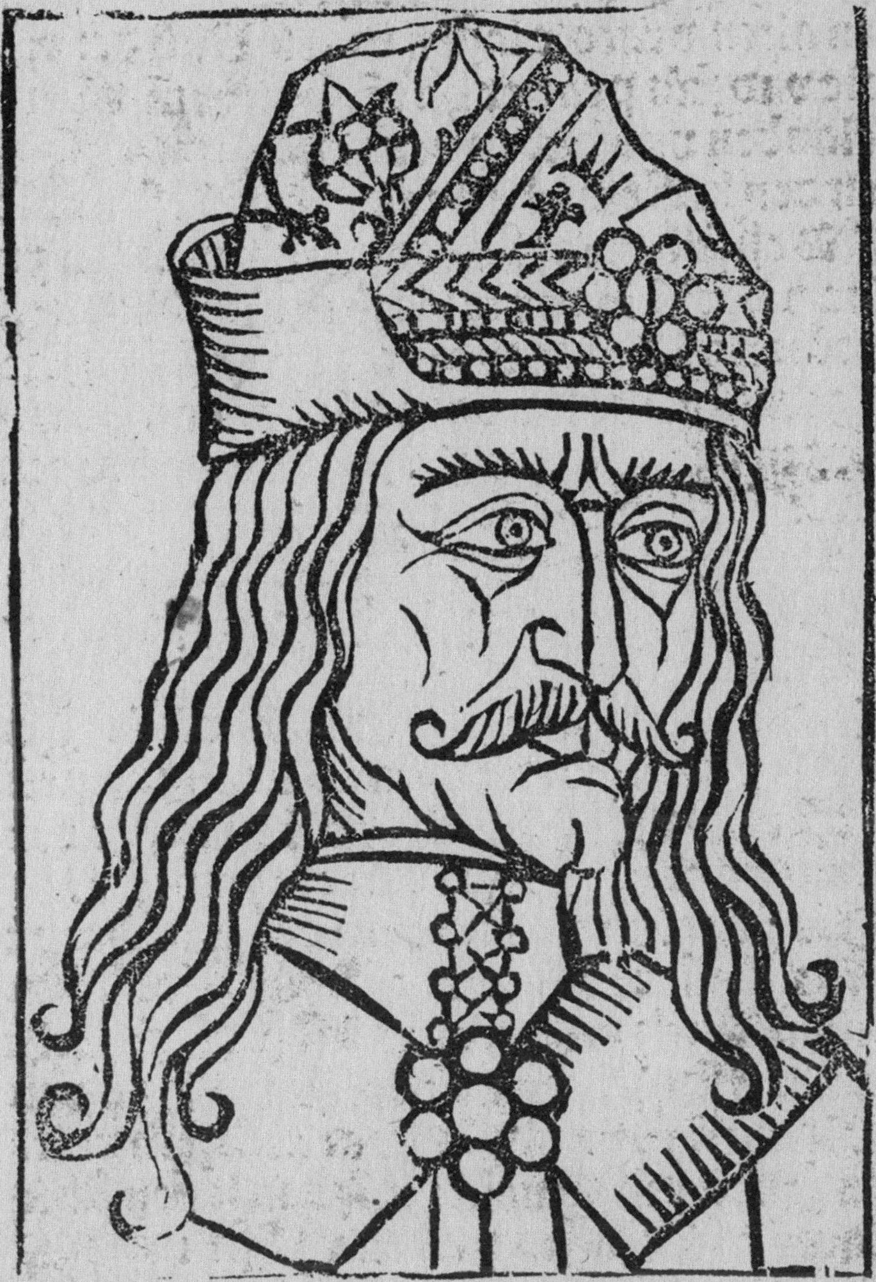

Dark Tourism

In late 2012, villagers in Zarožje, Serbia, started once again lining their pockets with garlic and carrying stakes because the old water mill — the former home of a local, legendary vampire named Sava Savanović — collapsed. They feared that the collapse of the mill meant Savanović would awaken to find a new place to rest. In the meantime, at the instruction of the municipal council, they needed to be on their guard. Before its collapse, tour groups were often allowed to visit the mill, so many suggest the council's warning was a ploy to bring more tourists to the area. Whatever the case, there were no reports of vampire attacks, and the mill has since been repaired and renovated. Maybe their precautions worked, and Savanovic, appeased by the repairs, sleeps again.

Vampires and Decomposition

◆◆◆

As it turns out, Dr. Van Helsing was correct about medical science explaining vampires, but not in the way he hoped. The Serbians digging up corpses and finding signs of vampirism were doing their best to explain natural processes like decomposition and the spread of disease without the framework of modern medicine that exists today.

In hindsight, the unusual bodies they exhumed were likely not unusual at all. Decomposition of interred bodies happens much more slowly than most people would expect. Putrefaction, which is defined as the decomposition of organic material due to microbial activity, occurs underground at a rate that is eight times slower relative to the surface. At a burial depth of just four feet (1 m), a corpse will retain most of its tissue for about a year. This is because the temperature is usually significantly lower underground relative to the open air, and the body is more protected from animal and insect activity. So, given that Flückinger was exhuming bodies of the recently deceased in Medvegia in January, likely in freezing or near-freezing temperatures, at which putrefaction effectively stops, it's no surprise they still seemed pretty fresh weeks or even months after their deaths.

That doesn't mean the bodies of suspected vampires weren't still decomposing, though, and we have to account for vampire encounters that happened outside of winter. Conveniently, the other signs of vampirism noted are actually signs of putrefaction at work:

- **"Fresh" blood around the mouth:** One of the main events as the body decomposes—and fair warning, this is gross—is that the lungs, brain, and other organs start to liquify. Natural swelling then pushes the resulting dark red, blood-like fluid out of the mouth and other orifices.

- **Groaning and "bleeding":** The swelling during putrefaction is likely also the cause of the groaning sound produced when a suspected vampire was staked — it was just a sudden release of gasses being forced out of the wound and past the vocal cords. The "blood" coming out of the wound was the same organ juice mentioned above.

- **Growth of hair and nails:** The hair and nail growth was not growth at all, but appeared as such because the skin around the follicles or fingers retracted as it started to dehydrate. Retraction of the gums for the same reason may have also created the illusion of elongated canines, or fangs, in some individuals.

As for the nighttime visitations reported by supposed victims of the original vampires, I'd venture that they were simply the result of superstitious minds running wild during episodes of sleep paralysis or perhaps due to hallucinations brought on by fevers. We've said it before and we'll say it again — brains are weird.

The Modern Vampire

People who regularly drink blood exist in the modern world, many of whom identify as vampires. You could have a friend or a coworker who identifies as a vampire.

But before you panic, know that self-identified vampires are not skulking around corners, lurking in alleyways, or ready to pounce and suck your blood. The only thing the members of this blood-drinking community have in common with the well-known folkloric vampire is their diet. These vampires retrieve their blood through a consensual interaction that often resembles that of a medical blood draw. Some drink blood as an attempt to gain psychic powers, but many believe that drinking blood helps treat vitamin deficiencies or other physiological ailments for which they've received no official medical diagnosis.

In interviews, some modern vampires have even said that their need for blood could be psychosomatic. Dr. Tomas Ganz at the University of California, Los Angeles, believes that the relief people feel from drinking blood is likely psychological. He says the combination of the ritual, the uniqueness of the substance (when compared to other food and drink), and the nutrition of blood can all play a part in offering relief to people with digestive or mental struggles.

Diagnosing Vampires

◆◆◆

In addition to a misunderstanding of natural decay processes, there are also specific diseases and medical conditions that may be behind folklore about vampire characteristics and/or were the cause of suspected vampire infestations. In the eighteenth and nineteenth centuries, outbreaks of plague and other highly infectious diseases were an ongoing threat, but there was a lack of understanding as to how these diseases spread, as well as a great deal of superstition about them. The disease with the strongest connections to outbreaks of vampirism is tuberculosis (TB), but people also link vampirism to outbreaks of infectious diseases such as rabies, pellagra, and cholera, noninfectious ones like porphyria and leukemia, and even mental health conditions like schizophrenia.

Tuberculosis

Known also as consumption, TB causes its victims to physically waste away, becoming thin and pale, and, of course, there's the whole coughing up blood thing. Outbreaks of TB would often take out entire households, with family members falling ill one after the other.

It was an outbreak of TB that led to the Great New England Vampire Panic of the late 1800s, where suspected vampires were again exhumed to check for telltale signs of nocturnal, bloodsucking activities, and in this case, sometimes had their lungs and heart removed and burned to stop them.

No one had conceived yet that a microscopic organism could be responsible for spreading this terrible illness, and people therefore turned to a supernatural explanation, in which earlier, deceased victims of the disease were rising from the dead to feed off the life force of their living family members.

RABIES

In the case of rabies, symptoms such as the urge to attack or bite, hypersensitivity to sunlight, aversion to strong smells (garlic, anyone?), and other delirious, irrational behavior could have been mistaken as supernatural in origin and subsequently attached to vampires. This is supported by the fact that older Slavic folklore does not distinguish between vampires and werewolves (it's easy to imagine that people encountered rabid wolves), and there were a large number of rabies cases recorded in Eastern Europe in the 1720s, around the time when the Serbian "vampires" emerged. That said, we'll come back to why this explanation is problematic in our discussion of werewolves (see page 90).

PORPHYRIA

Porphyria, also known as the "vampire disease," is not an infectious disease, but a debilitating group of genetic metabolic disorders that cause organic compounds called porphyrins to excessively accumulate in a person's body. Porphyrins are typically incorporated into heme, a major component of hemoglobin, the protein in red blood cells responsible for ferrying oxygen through the bloodstream.

Several types of porphyria cause extreme sensitivity to sunlight to the point where sufferers' skin will quickly blister and scar after exposure. Accumulation of porphyrins can also appear as red discoloration of teeth, bones, and urine, which others may have taken as a sign that the afflicted individual was drinking blood.

It is worth noting, however, that porphyria is exceedingly rare and not associated with violent behavior. It's possible there were concentrations of cases in remote areas where the gene pool was a bit more restricted that contributed to a few vampire stories, but it's certainly not a catchall diagnosis.

CATALEPSY

A final, and perhaps the most terrifying, possibility when it comes to vampire science and diseases is that the bodies of some "vampires" who were exhumed displayed odd characteristics because they were accidentally buried alive while in a comatose state by people hastily trying to avoid contagion. Catalepsy, a neurological condition related to diseases such as epilepsy, Parkinson's disease, and schizophrenia, causes the affected person to enter a catatonic state, during which they cannot move, their heart rate and respiration slow dramatically, and they become pale and completely unresponsive.

The condition usually lasts no more than a few minutes to a few hours, but in rare cases, can persist for days. Without modern medical equipment, and nearly undetectable heartbeat and breathing, it's no surprise some were assumed to be dead, and I'll let you imagine how it went for them when they woke up six feet (2 m) under.

WEREWOLVES

Stories about werewolves, or at least creatures that fall under the general definition of werewolves today, are ancient. What many consider the first recorded werewolf story appears in one of the earliest written texts, the *Epic of Gilgamesh* (ca. 2100 BCE), in which the title character refuses to become the lover of the goddess Ishtar because of her poor treatment of previous male companions. In particular, one of those men had been a shepherd who she spitefully turned into a wolf after a breakup in order to make him the enemy of his own flock and dogs. (To which I say, go off, girl—he probably deserved it.) Over 1,500 years later in Ancient Greece, historian and philosopher Herodotus wrote of a nomadic tribe from Scythia (now part of Russia) called the Neuri, who would transform into wolves for several days out of the year. In reality, they were likely just using wolf pelts for warmth, but superstition from outsiders turned them into shape-shifting monsters.

A few decades later, the Greek philosopher Plato wrote in his *Republic* of a religious cult in Arcadia (a historical region of the Peloponnesian Peninsula in southern Greece) who worshiped a wolfish form of Zeus known as Lycaean Zeus. His work and later writings by noted scholars Pliny the Elder and Pausanias indicate that the Arcadians practiced human and animal sacrifice rituals that ended with cooking and eating the meat of both animal and man. Those who indulged in human flesh would be transformed into wolves.

King Lycaon, a mythical character in Plato's writing fabricated to explain the origins of these strange customs, was also featured in later Latin texts by Ovid (*Metamorphoses*) and Hyginus (*Fabulae*) that expanded on his story.

As you might have guessed, Lycaon's name is where we get the term "lycanthropy."

How to Make a Werewolf

Beyond the classical world, werewolf (or more broadly, "shape-shifter") myths are fairly ubiquitous. Because of this, there are a wide variety of reasons people came up with as to why someone might become a werewolf. People today are most familiar with the idea that being bitten by a werewolf is a surefire way to be infected yourself, but the idea of werewolfism as a contagion spread by a bite is mainly (if not completely) derived from Hollywood depictions of werewolves, namely 1941's *The Wolf Man*.

In folklore, becoming a werewolf was primarily the result of a curse, either handed down as a divine punishment or bestowed by a witch, or due to a specific set of conditions being met. For example, werewolves could be people who were conceived under a new moon or who just happened to sleep under a full moon on a Wednesday or a Friday.

Sometimes the change into a werewolf or other animal was involuntary, but sometimes it was a choice. An Icelandic piece of literature from the thirteenth century called the *Völsunga Saga* features a pair of men donning wolf skins and being transformed into wolves, which could be linked to the real-life Norse berserkers who wore bear skins in battle and were known to be particularly fierce warriors, possibly fueled by hallucinogenic mushrooms. Later stories from the Middle Ages indicated that a belt made from a wolf skin was enough to facilitate the transformation.

And it's not just wolves that people can turn into, either, depending on where you look. For example, Africa has stories of people who transformed into hyenas or crocodiles. In China, some people could become tigers, and in Japan, foxes. Russian folklore tells of people who could turn into bears.

WOLVES AND WITCHES

◆◆◆

During the Middle Ages (500–1400 CE) and Early Modern Period (1500–1800 CE) in Europe, fear of werewolves went hand in hand with a fear of witchcraft, and hunts for them happened alongside witch hunts, although they were caught and prosecuted in much smaller numbers, and hunts were typically confined to specific regions. At the time, those who were accused and subsequently executed as werewolves were often considered to be practicing witchcraft or under the control of a witch. Witches and werewolves (and for that matter, vampires) were essentially seen as one and the same in the eyes of the Christian church and its followers, given that they were all thought to be derived from witchcraft and devilry.

In France, werewolves were known as *loup-garous*, and it has been proposed that up to thirty thousand people were accused of werewolfism in that country alone, although it's likely that figure is greatly exaggerated given that it is sourced from a book published in 1611 by a werewolf prosecutor named Pierre de Lancre, who was definitely pumping up his numbers.

Various other countries, including Germany, Switzerland, the Netherlands, and more, hosted werewolf trials throughout the fifteenth, sixteenth, and seventeenth centuries. As with witch trials happening at the time, those accused tended to be members of marginalized or vulnerable groups, such as the poor, immigrants, or those with mental health issues. Unfortunately, humanity has always loved finding a scapegoat for its problems.

The Wisconsin Werewolf

The Beast of Bray Road (a.k.a. The Wisconsin Werewolf) was first spotted on Bray Road in Jefferson, Wisconsin, United States, in 1936 by Mark Shackleton. The beast was spotted hunched over on all fours, digging like a canine; but when Shackleton approached the wolflike creature it stood up on its hind legs and snarled before running away. The beast gained popularity in the 1980s and 1990s with an increase in sightings (primarily around Elkhorn, Wisconsin); many reported the beast "acting aggressively", but it did not attack.

Physical descriptions vary by report, but it has been described by some as a five- to six-foot-tall (1.5–2 m) canid-looking beast with thick fur; later sightings liken the creature to a furry muscular-looking man. Linda Godfrey, author of *The Beast of Bray Road: Tailing Wisconsin's Werewolf*, believed the sightings were a mix of hoaxes, misidentifications of wildlife in Wisconsin where big cats, wolves, and bears can all be found, or sightings of something else completely. Whatever the creature is, it seems to have found its forever home in the Midwest.

YOU HUNT ME, I HUNT YOU

If we consider the science behind werewolf folklore, at the most basic level is the fact that humanity has feared real wolves for a long time. Our species initially encountered them around 140,000 years ago when we first left Africa, and early on, the risk of predation by these animals was a real concern (at least in the minds of prehistoric peoples, whether or not the wolves followed through). And it wasn't just the wolves we are familiar with today. Up until about twelve thousand years ago in the Americas, humans also had to contend with dire wolves, another type of canid that was similar in size to modern gray wolves, but with larger teeth, a more powerful jaw, and bulkier bodies (and yes, I *would* still pet that dog). Given our long history together, and our fear of them, it seems only natural that wolves (and possibly other large canids) appear frequently in our folklore.

We can see an association between real wolves and tales about their monstrous counterparts in the fact that there was a major decline in werewolf trials as real wolves were eradicated across many parts of Europe. In England, wolves disappeared during the reign of Henry VII (ca. 1485–1509), and in Scotland, the last wolf was believed to have been killed in 1680. Werewolf trials continued to happen for significantly longer in places like Germany and France, where wolves weren't completely gone until the late nineteenth and early twentieth centuries, respectively. Luckily, these beautiful creatures are now making a comeback in both countries, and although we know today that wolves are generally harmless to humans, I'd challenge you to listen to a recording of wolf howls and vocalizations and tell me you don't feel at least a shiver of primal fear.

Diagnosing Werewolves: Diseases

Like with vampires, werewolf folklore has been linked to various diseases. A common, and unsurprising, illness invoked to explain werewolf legends is rabies. Rabid animals often display an unnatural lack of fear toward humans, and I can easily imagine a scenario where someone might have mistaken that to mean a wolf wasn't just a regular wolf. If a person was then bitten by this wolf, and later started to display strange symptoms, including acting violently toward those around them, it's easy to see why their peers may have jumped to supernatural conclusions.

The possible connection between rabid wolves and werewolves was also noted back in the seventeenth century by German physician Daniel Sennert. However, this explanation likely only works for more rural and isolated communities because rabies has been a known disease in animals and humans for at least four thousand years, including the fact that it is spread through bites. Even in the seventeenth century, most people would have been able to recognize it for what it was.

About twenty years before porphyria was ever linked to vampire myths, it was suggested as a source of werewolf legends. Like with vampirism, there is an overlap between symptoms of the disease and werewolf traits, but again, they're not the smoking gun some portray them to be. People with porphyria are extremely sensitive to sunlight, so they might have preferred to come out only at night. Patients who did brave the daylight faced progressive scarring and disfigurement of their face and other exposed skin, which may have appeared to outsiders as if they were changing form or recovering from a rough night of werewolfing around town. In some forms of the disease, areas exposed to sunlight can start to grow excessive amounts of hair, a condition known as hypertrichosis. Hypertrichosis can also occur on its own due to a genetic mutation on the X-chromosome and is sometimes called "werewolf syndrome."

But let's be clear: Neither porphyria nor hypertrichosis turns people into rampaging beasts, and their symptoms are ongoing, unlike the temporary transformations described in werewolf stories. Furthermore, the appearance of people with hypertrichosis aligns more with Hollywood's version of werewolves than with traditional folklore, and there are no trial records that describe particularly hairy defendants during the time of werewolf hunts. This doesn't mean that porphyria and hypertrichosis didn't inspire the odd werewolf story throughout the ages, especially given people's tendency to fear the unfamiliar, but we should be careful not to stigmatize those currently living with these disorders.

Diagnosing Werewolves: Psychology

That brings us to the psychology of werewolves and a peculiar, exceedingly rare disorder known as clinical lycanthropy, in which a person believes themselves to be an animal (but not necessarily a wolf!). The fourth edition of the *Diagnostic and Statistical Manual of Mental Disorders* (or *DSM-IV*; we're on *DSM-5* now) actually included it as an official diagnosis. Today, it is categorized as a type of delusional misidentification syndrome (or DMS). Imaging of the brains of people with DMS show unusual activity in the portions associated with self-recognition and self-perception.

Interestingly, clinical lycanthropy was described and diagnosed as a type of melancholic depression or mania as far back as the fifth century by Byzantine physicians. At that time, sufferers were said to go out at night and frequent graveyards, where they behaved as if they were wolves. They were described as pale and haggard in appearance, with wounds on their legs from frequent stumbling, suffering from extreme thirst.

As few as fifty cases of clinical lycanthropy have been recorded since the Middle Ages, so it is certainly not a major source of werewolf tales, but it is potentially associated with several high-profile judicial cases involving accused werewolves. The most famous of these is a German man named Peter Stübbe (also appears spelled as Stumpp, Stump, Stumpf, and others). A pamphlet published in 1590 describes in lurid detail how Stübbe spent twenty-five years terrorizing the small village of Bedburg, Germany, where he mutilated livestock and murdered over a dozen men, women, and children, ripping them apart and sometimes sexually assaulting his victims or eating portions of the bodies. When Stübbe was finally hunted down and captured by a group of men and their dogs, they claimed they watched him shift back into a man from his wolf form. Under at least the threat of torture, Stübbe confessed to his crimes and said he transformed into a wolf to commit them by donning a belt of wolfskin that was gifted to him by the devil, and his fate was sealed.

Of course, as these things usually go, there was no concrete evidence linking Stübbe to these crimes beyond his confession given under duress, and he would go on to be brutally tortured and executed on October 31, 1589. Whether Stübbe was actually the killer he confessed to be or a scapegoat for a terrified town as some suspect he was, we can't know for sure. And we can't presume to diagnose him with a rare psychiatric disorder from over four hundred years in the future. It seems clear in this and cases like his, though, that the werewolf aspect may have been a way for people to justify how a person could commit these terrible crimes. It was much easier to swallow that the person wasn't actually a person rather than accept the darker side of human nature.

A final note on Stübbe: Both his daughter and his mistress were also executed for the simple "crime" of being associated with him, which, in the end, makes you wonder who the real monsters were.

These Kids are *Not* Alright

In the interest of ending on a lighter note (something that we often fail to do on the podcast), the last connection between medical science and werewolf folklore that I want to mention, which I find equal parts compelling and delightful, is that the stories were meant as metaphors for puberty. As many parents can probably tell you, teenagers can be a bit intense, and perhaps that's sometimes scary enough that people needed a monster to explain their behavior.

If you think about it, a surprising number of physical and hormonal changes during adolescence bear more than a passing resemblance to many features of werewolf folklore. These include increased aggression, rapid growth and muscle development, body hair in new places or in more abundance, and strong sexual urges. In seventeenth-century Guernsey, which is an island off the coast of France, the citizens took to referring to groups of teenagers who were out late at night and acting, well, like teenagers, as werewolves.

BOGEYMAN

If there's any supernatural entity in this world that is universal, it's probably the bogeyman (also appears as boogeyman, boogieman, bogyman, bogey, and other regional variants). Not only does nearly every culture have folklore about a bogeyman-like creature, but a large number of individuals also have their own personal versions. The bogeyman is the monster under the bed, the shadow that chases you up the stairs after you turn off the lights, and the terrifying creature that snatches the village children in the woods. In short, it is the personification of fear itself.

Because bogeyman stories are so widespread, we cannot nail down a single folkloric or historical origin for them. In all likelihood, the bogeyman has been around in one form or another since our species developed the ability to tell scary stories—like diamonds, fear is forever. There are a number of traits, though, that are common to a variety of bogeyman stories across cultures, including that they can shape-shift or are shapeless, they appear at night, they are often interested in eating human flesh, and most importantly, they are a tool used to deliberately frighten people, usually children.

WHAT'S IN A NAME?

In the English-speaking world, the word bogeyman first appeared in the sixteenth century in reference to trouble-causing, and sometimes malevolent, creatures known as hobgoblins. The root, bogey, is most commonly linked to the Middle English word *bogge* or *bugge*, which can be translated generally to mean "frightening specter," but was also used more specifically to mean bugbear, hobgoblin, or even scarecrow. Similar words appeared across Europe: The Germans had *bögge* (meaning hobgoblin), the Scottish had *bogle* (meaning hobgoblin or bugbear), and the Welsh had *bwg* (meaning ghost or hobgoblin). Notably, bugbears are bogey figures linked to the earlier *Bugibu*, a demon from a French poem written in the twelfth century. Alternative, but less likely, etymologies suggested for bogeyman include a nickname for Napoleon Bonaparte (Old Boney or Boneyman) that was used to frighten British children, a reference to Bugis pirates (bugismen) encountered by European sailors in Indonesia and Malaysia, or a variation on the Buggy Men that were sent around with carts to pick up deceased plague victims.

A Bogeyman for the Digital Age

Slenderman—a modern, digital-age bogeyman created via Photoshop in 2009 by Eric Knudsen as an entry to a paranormal photoshop contest—gained popularity in the early 2010s. The Slenderman mythos has evolved over time, but he is commonly portrayed as either a "dark guardian" to help protect children from abusive families and bullies, or as a killer who feeds on young children. Some Slenderman content is purposely presented as reality (e.g., found-footage videos, photoshopping historical photos, etc.); and while the majority of adults recognize Slenderman as a fictional being, children, who have become the target audience for the games, literature, or art, are far more likely to believe in his existence. A child's belief can be so strong that they bring Slenderman to life. This is especially true for vulnerable children who turn to Slenderman (or similar ideas) for protection, friendship, or a sense of belonging.

The Science of Boogie

While the exact folkloric origins of the bogeyman are difficult or impossible to suss out, there are clear reasons for its existence from a scientific perspective. One I've already mentioned is that the bogeyman is simply a tool used by anxious parents to keep their children safe. Humans have an inherent, evolutionary drive to keep our offspring from harm, and historically that might have come at the expense of traumatizing our kids a bit with monster stories.

I know this seems a bit barbaric given our modern knowledge of child psychology, and far from the realm of the gentler form of parenting most of us strive for today, but in historical times with significantly higher child mortality rates, desperate times may have called for desperate measures. This also helps to explain regional and cultural variation in bogeymen figures, as each one reflects the specific concerns of a given area and time.

And even then, children are perfectly able to create their own bogeymen. Between the ages of two and six, kids' imaginations come alive. This means we see the emergence of many common fears, such as fear of the dark, as well as the invention of not only imaginary friends but imaginary monsters, too.

It's totally normal for children to have irrational fears at these ages, and it's important for their development. After all, it's an innate sense of fear that helps keep us alive on a day-to-day basis. Kids have to start from scratch and learn what it even means to be afraid and what they should reasonably be afraid of. Creating a bogeyman is a way children can contextualize their irrational fears into things that they can then learn to process and overcome. An unlucky few, however, may have vanquished their childhood bogeyman only to have it show back up during their teenage or early adult years thanks to sleep paralysis. Sometimes you just can't win.

Something Spooky

Growing up, my family had a shared bogeyman—what started as a friend of my brother's became a bizarre nightmare for my parents. It all began when my brother started hanging out with his new (imaginary) friend. According to my brother (at the time), this friend was a thirty-five-year-old man who was living in the basement of my parents' house, and he went by New-me (or Knew-Me). When my brother, who is six years my senior, started kindergarten, he met new friends, and left New-me behind.

Over the next five or six years, I was born, and my family moved into a new house. New-me was all but forgotten, as it had been several years since anybody had talked to or about him. One day I began talking to a new (imaginary) friend. When I introduced this friend to my parents, I introduced him as none other than New-me. Neither my brother nor I have any memory of our time spent "hanging out" with New-me (or any imaginary friends), but when recently asked about it, my mom replied, "New-me was a part of our lives for a long time."

Test Your Knowledge

Monster Madness

Each of the two statements below includes a short description or a fun fact about one of our favorite monsters. For each, guess what monster the statement applies to.

A. This literary monster, made by assembling body parts of corpses, was the star of the first major science fiction novel. The story of the monster's creation was influenced by two important scientific learnings of the early nineteenth century: the discovery of resuscitation and the theory of galvanism—the idea that electrical current could be used to reanimate the dead and stimulate life.

B. The subject of countless modern movies and video games, these undead, infectious, ravenous monsters address the fears of pandemic spread and an apocalyptic world. The chaotic scenes depicted in these monster movies are examples of what happens when societal systems break down, which are far more common during times of economic stress. The first literary references to these monsters were seen as early as the seventeenth century, but they gained popularity after the release of George Romero's 1968 film *Night of the Living Dead*.

Answers on page 201

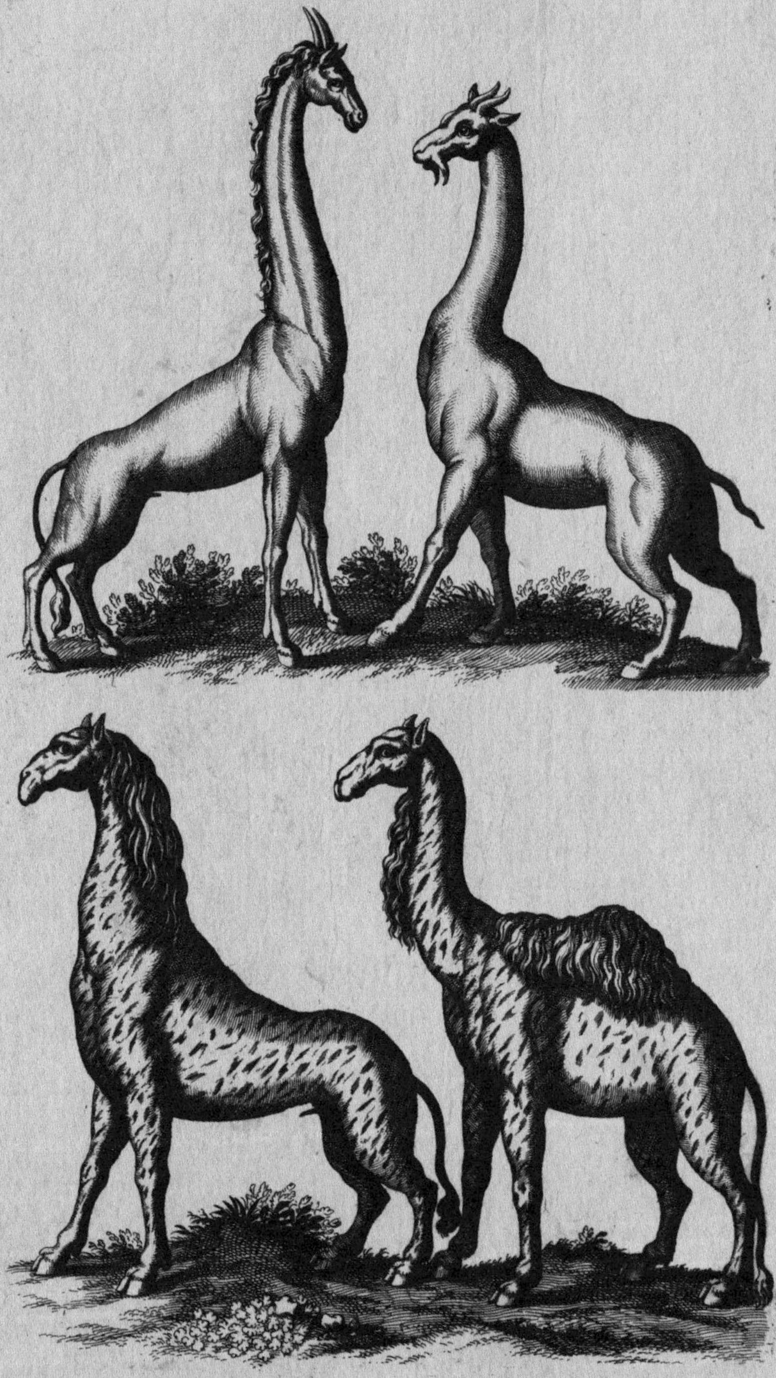

CRYPTIDS

Today, cryptids and cryptozoology (the study of cryptids) have come to represent an innate desire most of us have that there is still some mystery left in this world hidden away in wild, unspoiled places. And that hope is not necessarily unfounded. Several hundred new species are discovered each year, and we're not just talking about small ones like insects or fish. Additionally, there are animals that are accepted by science today that used to be considered cryptids. Other animals that were presumed to be extinct and then rediscovered, are referred to as Lazarus taxons. But as the remote parts of the world become fewer and farther between, so too do our chances of ever proving the existence of any of the current cryptids. In this section, we'll explore the history of three legendary cryptic creatures and examine what science says about their feasibility and the possibility that they'll ever be found.

WHAT IS A CRYPTID?

Although the word "cryptids" is a modern one, first appearing no earlier than the 1940s, the practice of supplementing known animals with fantastical ones dates back hundreds, if not thousands, of years. Many creatures that we consider legendary monsters today were cryptids until biology and exploration caught up with them.

In the sixteenth century, Conrad Gesner, a Swiss naturalist who is known as the founder of modern zoology, included animals like dragons, mermaids, and unicorns in his five-volume compendium *Historiae animalium*. At the time, their existence was based on mistaken or exaggerated observations of animals like snakes, manatees, and antelopes or rhinos, respectively (and among others).

In simple terms, cryptids are animals that are rumored to exist, but are not recognized by mainstream science. They are creatures, sometimes out of folklore or myth, for which we only have "cryptic" evidence of their existence, meaning that it is indirect or anecdotal (for example, eyewitness accounts, footprints, and ambiguous photos or videos), as opposed to direct evidence (for example, live specimens, bodies, or bones). Cryptids can be divided into three primary categories, and there can be crossover between them. These categories are:

- **Animals that are "out of time":** These cryptids are thought to be remnant populations of animals that science says went extinct anywhere from decades to millions of years ago.

- **Animals that are "out of place":** An animal that is observed far outside of its regular habitat, but that we can't find conclusive evidence for, can be considered a cryptid. For example, for years people have claimed they've seen large cats that look similar to panthers in Britain.

- **Mythical "animals":** These are the cryptids that are less plausible biologically. This includes hybrids of more than one type of animal, such as the Jersey Devil, or monstrous ones like the chupacabra. It also includes cryptids that are exaggerated versions of real animals. For example, the Kraken may have been inspired by giant squid sightings.

BIGFOOT

In North America, no other cryptid looms quite as large (or as hairy) as bigfoot. The popular consensus is that bigfoot is a remnant of a thought-to-be extinct great ape species, or more specifically, an unknown hominid that has persisted alongside humans as one of the more plausible cryptids. Heck, even famed primatologist Jane Goodall said she wouldn't rule out their existence.

You might be surprised to learn that bigfoot started out as a supernatural shape-shifter, and much of the imagery and behavior we associate with this beloved cryptid today comes from just a few questionable sources. So how did we go from supernatural wild men to the giant ape we know and love today, and how likely is it that there's an undiscovered primate out in the woods somewhere?

SASQUATCH, THE SHAPE-SHIFTER

The story of bigfoot began in the ancient forests of the Harrison River Valley in British Columbia, Canada, where the Sts'ailes people have been telling stories of encounters with a large, shapeshifting, supernatural being known as *sasq'ets* (translates to "hairy man" or "wild man") for thousands of years. Early newspaper clippings from the region about sightings of this creature date back to 1884, but it was thrust into the mainstream in 1929 when *Maclean's* magazine published an article titled "Introducing B.C.'s Hairy Giants." The article was written by a Canadian government agent named John W. Burns, who called the creatures "sasquatch," an anglicized version of the original *sasq'ets*. The name obviously stuck, and sightings of sasquatch continued in the area.

In 1957, the village council from a small town called Harrison Hot Springs (host to an annual Sasquatch Days festival since 1938) had the bright idea to apply for federal funding to host a sasquatch hunt in honor of the British Columbia Centennial. Their funding request was unfortunately not approved, but there was widespread news coverage of the bid around the world, and the committee responsible for reviewing Centennial celebration proposals ended up advertising a $5,000 reward to anyone who could capture and bring a sasquatch in alive.

SASQUATCH GOES APE

It was in light of the newfound popularity of sasquatch in Harrison Hot Springs that a man named William Roe stepped forward in 1957 to share his story of an encounter from two years earlier, which went on to become what many consider the single most important sighting of the creature to have ever occurred. Roe claimed that while he was out hunting, he came across a large animal in a clearing and was able to sit and observe it for some time. According to his description, the sasquatch had apelike facial features, was six feet (2 m) tall and broadly muscled, covered in dark brown hair, and had breasts, indicating it was female. Other details included broad feet, long arms that reached almost to her knees, and a thick, short neck. The encounter ended when the sasquatch noticed Roe's presence and rapidly walked out of the clearing, looking back over her shoulder at him as she went. (Keep this detail in mind—it will be important later.)

Roe's physical description of sasquatch became the standard for nearly all future sightings, and importantly, solidified it as an apelike creature, whereas some earlier stories described the creature as unusually large, but mostly human in appearance. Here's the thing about Roe, though: It appears that he didn't speak to anyone about this supposed sighting for the two years between when it occurred and when the media circus kicked off in 1957. Furthermore, no one in the cryptozoology or scientific community ever met with him in person, there were no attempts to ascertain anything about his character, and we don't have any verification that he was even in the area at the time of his encounter.

These issues aside, to the cryptozoology community and the general public, Roe's encounter meant that sasquatch stepped its big, hairy feet fully out of the realm of the supernatural to become a real, flesh-and-blood animal traipsing about the Canadian wilderness.

Apes All Around!

Bigfoot is not the only suspected primate in the world of cryptozoology and is part of a group that is sometimes categorized as "cryptohominids." Oftentimes, they are considered one-and-the-same — just regional varieties of the same species that were able to spread around the world much like humans.

The Himalayas are home to the yeti, which I, like most people, thought was covered in white fur thanks to Hollywood depictions, but is actually described as having reddish, brown, or black fur. The white-furred version is from a reporter's mistranslation of a local name for the creature, Metoh Kangmi, which he took to mean "Abominable Snowman," and the film industry took to mean the yeti was white.

Elsewhere in Asia, you can find stories of bigfoot-like creatures called yeren and almas, and further afield in Australia, people have reported encounters with yowies since at least the 1820s. My personal favorite is the mapinguari from the Amazon rainforest of South America — a hairy, smelly, cyclops with a gaping mouth in the middle of its abdomen and feet turned backward. The mapinguari was sometimes grouped together with bigfoot as some sort of primate by early cryptozoologists but may actually be inspired by stories passed down from a time when prehistoric humans lived alongside giant ground sloths.

My, What Big Footprints You Have!

◆◆◆

In 1958, the creatures known as sasquatch became bigfoot after large footprints began showing up at logging road construction sites around Bluff Creek in California, United States. While similar in appearance to human footprints, they were enormous at around sixteen inches (41 cm) long and seven inches (18 cm) wide. The footprints were first noticed by a member of the logging crew named Jerry Crew, who arrived at work one morning in late August to find his bulldozer surrounded by them.

When he mentioned the tracks to his team, Crew was met with stories of strange occurrences (and accompanying footprints) at other worksites. The workers were understandably spooked and soon started blaming any mishap, act of vandalism, or loss of equipment on a creature they dubbed Big Foot. More tracks appeared a few weeks later, and Crew made his famous plaster casts of them.

On October 6, a front-page article about the footprints and other shenanigans appeared in the local paper, *The Humboldt Times*, which printed the mysterious footprint-leaver's name as Bigfoot. The story was then picked up by the Associated Press, appearing in the likes of *The New York Times* and *The Los Angeles Times*, and just as William Roe's encounter set the standard for the appearance of bigfoot, the Bluff Creek footprints launched the cryptid into the mainstream and helped make it the popular phenomenon it remains today.

But all was not as it seemed. In 2002, the family of a recently deceased man named Ray Wallace came forward, armed with pairs of wooden, oversized feet, to admit that he was the source of all the footprints around Bluff Creek. Wallace was the co-owner of the company in charge of the worksites where the prints were found, and brother to Shorty, Jerry Crew's foreman. He was also a known prankster, and as it turns out, was almost immediately considered a suspect when the original tracks appeared. He denied involvement at the time, but went on to perpetrate several additional hoaxes, including one where he was exposed as a fraud when he failed to deliver a juvenile bigfoot he claimed he captured.

Despite attempts by some bigfoot enthusiasts to cling to the notion that at least some of the Bluff Creek footprints were genuine (enter the unfalsifiable ad hoc hypothesis—maybe Wallace was just inspired by the original set . . . right?), it's clear that they do not hold up to scientific scrutiny and are, in all likelihood, a complete fabrication.

The Patterson-Gimlin Film

The Patterson-Gimlin film is the quintessential bigfoot footage that most of us are familiar with and is the source of the iconic pose with the creature in mid-stride, looking toward the camera. The one-minute-long film is named for the two former rodeo cowboys who recorded it, Roger Patterson and Bob Gimlin. In the fall of 1967, Patterson and Gimlin set out into the wilderness near Bluff Creek in California, United States, with the express purpose of capturing video evidence of bigfoot.

On October 20, the two men, who were on horseback, came around a bend in the river to find a large, hairy, apelike animal crouched next to the water. Patterson's startled horse reared, throwing him off, but he managed to grab his camera from a saddlebag and record just shy of sixty seconds of footage of a female bigfoot (who's since been nicknamed "Patty") walking away from him, turning her head once to look directly at the camera. After the encounter, Patterson and Gimlin also made several casts of footprints she left behind during her traverse across the riverbank.

The Patterson-Gimlin film has been the subject of fierce debate since it was first released to the public. The consensus of most among the scientific community is that it is a hoax, but to many bigfoot enthusiasts, including a few anthropologists, it is the single most compelling and most important piece of evidence in existence. I'm sure it won't surprise you to learn that I lean toward Team Hoax, but I admit that I am hard pressed to completely dismiss the footage, especially given that decades of scrutiny haven't been able to conclusively debunk it. So, let's review the evidence — we'll start with the reasons many believe Patty is the real deal:

- The muscle tone and visible movement of musculature beneath the skin, as well as the quality and texture of Patty's hair, are remarkably realistic. There are no visible seams or zippers. If it is a costume, it is a very good one for the time, and there have been several unsuccessful attempts to reproduce the footage using a suit.

- Patty is female with visible breasts, which apparently would be more difficult to fake in terms of appearance and movement.

- Some argue that Patty's gait and arm movements would be impossible, or at least very difficult, for a human to reproduce.

- The footprints that Patty left display a distinctive "pressure ridge" across the midfoot, which bigfoot proponent and anthropologist Jeff Meldrum suggests is evidence of a feature found only in nonhuman primates called a midtarsal break.

- Patterson went on to invest a significant amount of additional time, money, and effort into finding more evidence of bigfoot's existence in the years that followed. He maintained his famous film's authenticity until his death in 1972, and Bob Gimlin, who is still alive, has also never changed his story.

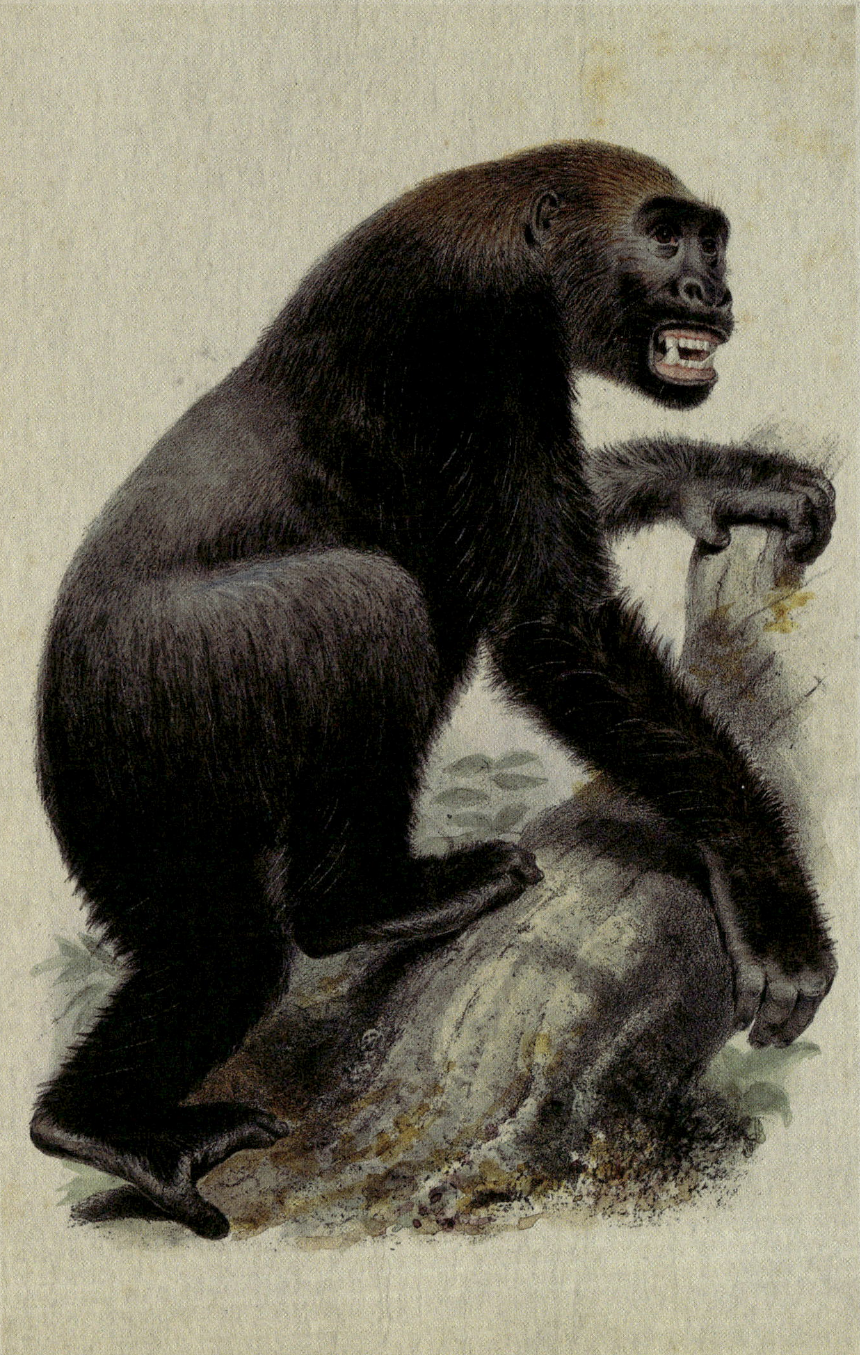

Now for a summary of the evidence put forth to suggest Patty was a hoax (including some counterpoints to the arguments above):

- Realistic muscle movement beneath a rubber suit could be accomplished using bags of water underneath the skin, and while it is tricky to get right, Patty's exaggerated walk has been emulated by people.

- The location of the distinctive mid-foot pressure ridge across the foot doesn't match what we'd expect for most hominids, for whom it is further back toward the heel.

- It is an extraordinary, dare I say near unbelievable, stroke of luck that on their first attempt, Patterson and Gimlin were able to capture clear (if a little shaky), out-in-the-open footage of a bigfoot. There are multiple seasons of multiple television shows dedicated to looking for bigfoot, and people have had access to 4K video on their phones for over a decade, and yet no one else has come close.

- It is also remarkably convenient that they were coincidentally down to their last bit of film for the day and could only capture the sixty seconds of footage we see, which ends right when Patty enters the woods.

- Patterson and Gimlin chose Bluff Creek as their target filming location because of the footprints and sightings that started happening in the 1950s, but we know now that the original footprints were likely a hoax.

- Patterson was involved in bigfoot projects before his 1967 trip to Bluff Creek. Most notably, in a book he wrote on the subject, he drew an illustration of William Roe's sasquatch encounter.

- Skeptics point out that Patterson's drawing bears a remarkable resemblance to the footage he would go on to capture at Bluff Creek, and even more suspicious is how closely that footage of Patty matches William Roe's description of events, from the fact that she was described as female to the look back at her observers as she walked away (See? I told you we'd come back to that!). Additionally, both Patterson/Gimlin and Roe claimed that despite having rifles with them, they couldn't bear to shoot the creature.

- Those who knew Roger Patterson indicated in interviews that his character and ambition were such that he would not have been above perpetrating a hoax. Also, the fact that he used his own money to continue searching for bigfoot in the years after filming Patty is somewhat less magnanimous when you consider he profited at least $100,000 for the film (equivalent to over $900,000 today). Why not keep the ruse going and try to make even more?

- A confession by a man named Bob Heironimus that he was the "man in the suit" was the focus of a 2004 book by Greg Long, *The Making of Bigfoot*. There is circumstantial evidence to support Heironimus' claim—he lived in the same town as Patterson and Gimlin and appeared in an earlier bigfoot film produced by Patterson—but it ultimately comes down to his word versus Bob Gimlin's, who maintains that the film is genuine.

Point being, if we can't take eyewitness accounts of bigfoot sightings as evidence to support a hypothesis that bigfoot exists, we also need to dismiss them when they go the other way. The only way to verify would be to have the Patterson-Gimlin suit in hand, which, if it ever existed, has seemingly been lost to time or destroyed. This also applies to claims made by costume makers that they created the suit for Patterson, and yet there is no concrete evidence, such as invoices or order forms, to back it up.

Bigfoot Today

Cryptozoologists and bigfoot enthusiasts are well aware of the issues and inconsistencies present in the supposed evidence of bigfoot's existence, and yet often choose to set aside scientific ideals to try to justify a way around them or just outright ignore them. For the public, who are less likely to be familiar with or look into the gritty details of these foundational stories, the proverbial train has left the station. Surveys indicate that up to 29 percent of Americans and 21 percent of Canadians believe in the existence of bigfoot, and new sightings are reported quite often. More than ten thousand encounters have been logged in the United States alone in the past fifty years, and at least once a year, a new video or image of a supposed bigfoot goes viral (although they are almost always blurry, obscured by darkness, or very obviously a mistaken identification of another large mammal). Bigfoot is clearly here to stay, but where does the science stand?

What Is Bigfoot?

If we want to establish a scientific search for bigfoot, the first step is to try to determine exactly what we're looking for. Eyewitness accounts describe an apelike animal that is, on average, eight to ten feet (2–3 m) tall, well-muscled, with medium to dark brown hair that is at least an inch or two (2.5 or 5 cm) long covering most of the body. That leaves us with a few options for what it might be, all of which exist in our evolutionary past.

The most common extinct primate linked to bigfoot is *Gigantopithecus blacki*, the largest known ape to ever exist, which lived in southern China, Vietnam, and India between about 2.5 million to 200,000 years ago. Interestingly, it was first discovered by a German paleoanthropologist named Ralph von Koenigswald, who came across its large molars being sold as medicinal dragon bones in a pharmacy in Hong Kong.

Gigantopithecus was the species preferred by famed anthropologist and bigfoot advocate, Grover Krantz, and from the physical description, it's not hard to see why. The extinct giant ape, which was a close relative of modern orangutans, stood about ten feet (3 m) tall when upright and weighed up to 1,200 pounds (544 kg). Because of its size, however, most scientists believe *Gigantopithecus* walked on its knuckles like orangutans and gorillas, although Krantz argued it was bipedal. Funny enough, one of the factors that may have ushered along the extinction of *Gigantopithecus* was competition with or overhunting by *Homo erectus*, an ancient hominid (one of us!) who is also mentioned as a possible bigfoot species.

Additional nonhominid species considered for bigfoot include members of the *Paranthropus* and *Australopithecus* genuses. A variety of other hominids have also been suggested, including Neanderthals, Denisovans, *Homo erectus*, *Homo heidelbergensis*, and *Homo gardarensis*. It's even been proposed that bigfoot is a variant of our own species that regressed to a more apelike form after being isolated for some time.

Note that these possibilities are also invoked when it comes to the other apelike cryptids around the world. Additionally, it is worth reacknowledging Indigenous stories when it comes to a discussion of other hominids as bigfoot or other apelike cryptids, because with oral histories that extend back for thousands of years, they may be remembering times when *Homo sapiens* coexisted with other hominid species.

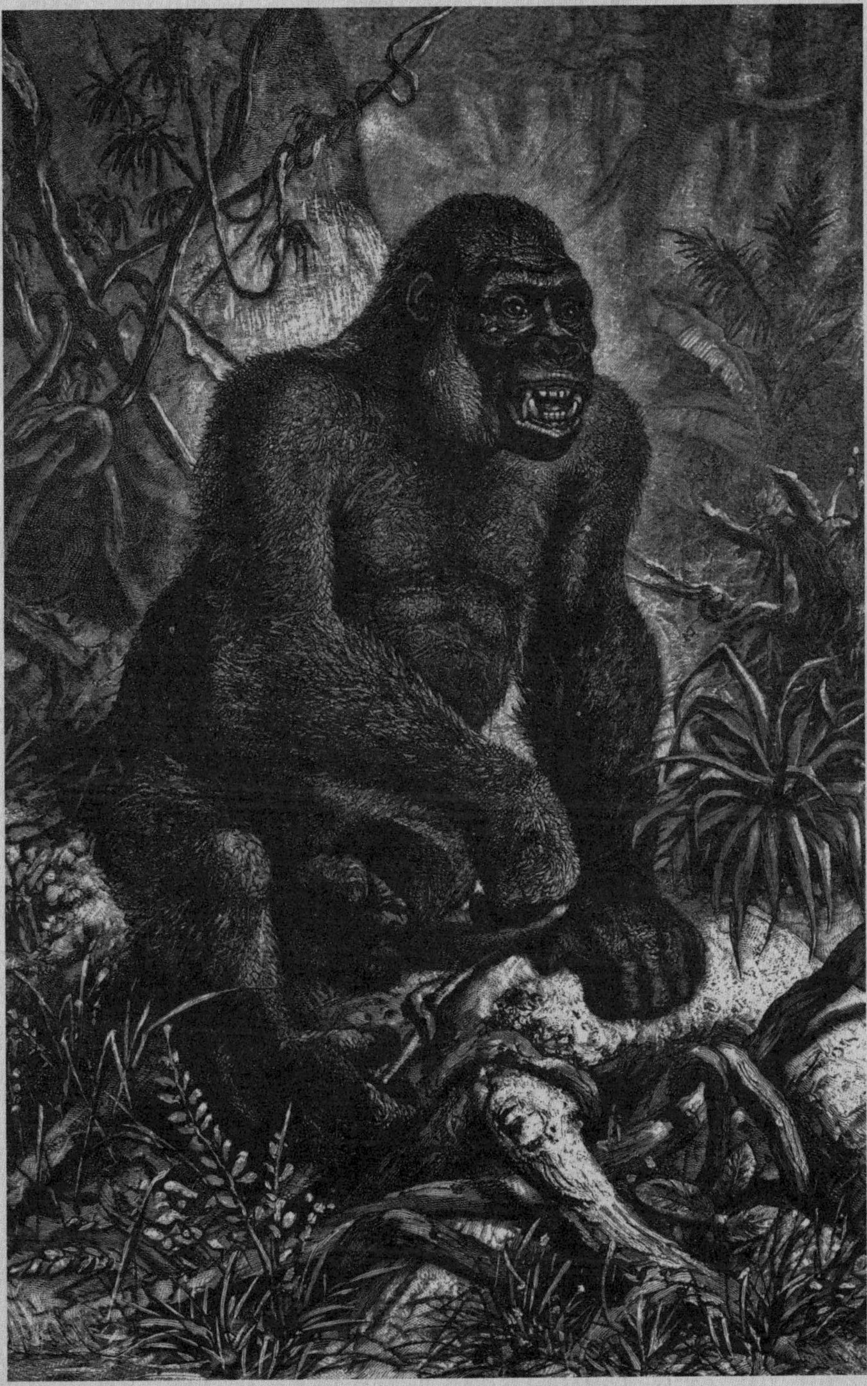

No Body, No Bigfoot

The suggestion that bigfoot is a remnant of an extinct primate species highlights a critical problem for the possibility of its existence, and that is the lack of physical evidence in the form of a body, or at least feces, hair, or some other bodily byproduct. In North America, there's not even fossil evidence of other hominid species. In an increasingly crowded world, it seems more and more unlikely that a large mammal unknown to science could exist alongside humans and have no bodies or other concrete physical evidence ever turn up, especially since it is one that people are actively searching for. Why hasn't some hunter stumbled across one in the woods, or an unlucky motorist hit one with their car?

For a population of extinct apes or hominids to persist for tens, if not hundreds, of thousands of years past their accepted extinction date, there have to be enough individuals to support a healthy breeding population. We're talking at least five hundred individuals for an isolated group, and yet there are endangered animals with comparatively small populations that we still regularly find signs of and are able to photograph. For example, mountain gorillas and Tapanuli orangutans are considered two of the most endangered species in the world, with only around six hundred and eight hundred individuals left in the wild, respectively.

The Scientific Search for Sasquatch

Two recent studies on the bigfoot phenomenon that were conducted and published within the bounds of mainstream science suggest that many sasquatch sightings and evidence are simply cases of mistaken identity. In 2012, a team of researchers at Oxford University (United Kingdom) and the Museum of Zoology (Lausanne, Switzerland) led by geneticist Brian Sykes put out a call for people to submit hair samples that were believed to have come from unknown primate specimens. They received fifty-seven samples from around the world, including various places in the United States, Russia, Indonesia, India, Bhutan, and Nepal.

Twenty of the samples were immediately rejected because they weren't hairs at all or were in too poor of a condition to analyze. Thirty-seven of them were processed for DNA and then compared to the DNA signatures of known animals, and probably to no one's surprise, all of them could be matched to existing animals. The most unusual were two from India and Bhutan that were a match to polar bears, which garnered some excitement that Himalayan bears might be some hybrid species, but alas, no unknown or extinct primates were found in the bunch (and yes, I can just hear bigfoot proponents arguing that the *real* sample was one of the ones too degraded to analyze).

More recently, a statistical study released in early 2024 compared the locations of sasquatch sightings with data on black bear populations and found significant overlap, meaning that the elusive ape, in many cases, may just be another bear in the woods. Previous studies identified correlations between bears and bigfoot in the Pacific Northwest, but the new study, conducted by data scientist Floe Foxon, was expanded to include all of the United States and Canada. Data on sasquatch sightings came from geotagged reports compiled by the Bigfoot Field Researchers Organization. These were overlaid in a statistical model with census data on the human population, estimates of the amount of forested area in each state or province, and data on bear populations.

Foxon found that for every one thousand bears in an area, the number of bigfoot sightings increased by 4 percent, and that you can expect about one bigfoot encounter per five thousand bears. Basically, more bears means people see more bigfoots. Logically, the bigfoot-bear correlation makes sense and has been recognized by skeptics for some time. Black bears can be a variety of colors (including brown or reddish brown), they are capable of standing on their hind legs and walking for a few steps, and they are of similar weight to bigfoots.

It's not just appearance, either. Bears are solitary creatures, active at night, can leave large scratches on trees, engage in vocalizations such as grunts, woofs, howls, and a variety of other noises similar to those described for bigfoot, are naturally curious about humans, and can be quite stinky. Combine some or all of this with a healthy dose of suggestibility and nerves, and you just might have yourself a bigfoot.

MOTHMAN

Our next cryptid, a winged humanoid known as Mothman, is decidedly more supernatural and less plausible as a flesh-and-blood animal. This creepy creature terrified a small West Virginia town for just over a year, culminating in a tragic accident that killed almost four dozen people. Mothman has been called a harbinger of doom by some, and a benevolent protector by others, or maybe he's just a strange bird that surprised some teenagers in the woods. Whatever the case, Mothman swooped into the hearts and minds of many to become one of the most beloved cryptids. But let's start from the beginning in the woods of rural West Virginia.

"BIRD . . . CREATURE . . . SOMETHING!"

Most people say the legend of Mothman started on a dark country road about seven miles (11 km) outside of the small town of Point Pleasant, West Virginia, United States, on November 15, 1966. That night at about 11:30 p.m., a young married couple, Roger and Linda Scarberry, were driving on State Route 62 with friends Steve and Mary Mallette. They were not far from the abandoned National Guard Armory building and power plant (within an area called the TNT area by locals because the site was used to manufacture and store munitions during World War II) when the four friends claimed they were confronted by a monstrous creature standing in the middle of the road.

The terrifying man-shaped specter stood six to seven feet (2 m) tall, with eyes that shone bright red in the headlights, and white or grayish wings (the light color is a detail that is often missing from modern depictions!) that were ten feet (3 m) across. Linda Scarberry also noted that the creature squeaked like a mouse, but stranger and more eerie sounding. Roger, who was driving, panicked and quickly turned the car around to begin speeding away. The creature gave chase—it was a clumsy runner, but eventually took flight and was able to keep pace with the car, even as it reached speeds of one hundred miles per hour (161 kph). (A speed, I'll note, I am skeptical of given that I live with a shameless number exaggerator—were they really going that fast?)

It pursued the vehicle until they reached the city limits—they all noted the monster seemed to be afraid of the lights—before turning back. The frightened teenagers eventually headed to the local police station that same night and relayed the whole incredible story. The next day, the police held a press conference and the local newspaper, *The Point Pleasant Register*, ran a story with the amazing headline, "Couples See Man-Sized Bird . . . Creature . . . Something!"

It's a Bird! It's an Insect! It's . . . Mothman!

News of the mysterious flying creature quickly spread across the United States, with one newspaper editor deeming it "Mothman" in a nod to the *Batman* series starring Adam West that premiered earlier that year. In response to the original article, reports of prior and subsequent sightings started rolling in. A group of five gravediggers reported they'd seen a winged humanoid fly over them three days before the Scarberrys' and Mallettes' encounter. Another resident came forward and claimed Mothman abducted their beloved German shepherd the day before the November 15 sighting—the dog reportedly ran off into the woods after a pair of glowing eyes and was never seen again.

After that, Mothman lurked outside peoples' houses and chased them inside, was observed perched at the edge of a quarry by a group of teenagers, and continued pursuing cars out of the TNT area. In total, about a hundred sightings happened in the thirteen months after the Scarberrys and Mallettes made their police report, and it wasn't just cryptid sightings plaguing Point Pleasant during that time. Reports of men in black, livestock mutilations, and more strange occurrences popped up over the following year.

Many theories floated around at the time of the sightings about the possible identity of Mothman. Some thought it might be an alien or a being from another dimension, while others speculated it was a mutant created by toxic material leftover from the munitions factory or power plant. Early skeptics dismissed it as the misidentification of a bird. Two firefighters who visited the TNT site three days after the initial sighting saw the unknown creature and were adamant it was a bird. Another local man shot a snowy owl that he believed was the culprit. Dr. Robert L. Smith, a professor of wildlife biology at West Virginia University, declared that the creature could be a sandhill crane due to its size and the red feathers around their eyes, but it had to be a lost one because they are not normally found in the area.

Mothman would achieve its final form on December 15, 1967, when disaster struck the town of Point Pleasant. That day, the Silver Bridge, a main thoroughfare out of town that spanned the Ohio River, collapsed, killing forty-six people after their cars plunged into the icy water below. Later, residents claimed they saw Mothman hovering above the doomed structure shortly before the accident. After the bridge collapse, Mothman sightings became few and far between, and then stopped entirely, leading to speculation that Mothman was a bad omen, a warning, or worse, the cause of the tragic event, and had since moved on.

The real culprit, of course, was a flaw in one of the suspension chains that inevitably failed after forty years of stress and corrosion. However, the idea of Mothman as an omen was immortalized in 1975 when paranormal journalist and ufologist (a term to describe someone who studies UFOs) John Keel wrote his famous book, *The Mothman Prophecies*. Since then, Mothman has continued to grow into the beloved cryptid we know today, with sightings happening in various places around the world (often associated with tragedies such as the Chernobyl disaster in Ukraine and 9/11 in the United States—he really gets around!), and the town of Point Pleasant hosting an annual Mothman Festival that is attended by over ten thousand fans.

The Science of Mothman

◆◆◆

There haven't been any true scientific inquiries into Mothman, given that this is a cryptid that primarily exists in the realm of folklore and the paranormal, but we can examine some of the factors that might explain from a scientific standpoint what the Scarberrys and Malletes saw and what led an entire town to start having visions of a large, winged humanoid. To start, it's important to note that most, if not all, skeptics agree that the two young couples saw *something* out in the woods that scared them the night of November 15. The most likely explanation is that it was a misidentification of another creature, and the flying necessitates a bird. The sandhill crane hypothesis is intriguing given their large wingspan and red heads, but they aren't nocturnal, Point Pleasant isn't part of their natural range, and Mothman was described as having little to no neck.

The better option is that the four teens were surprised by an owl. Joe Nickell, an investigator for the Committee for Skeptical Inquiry, considered a few different types, and landed on a barred owl because of its prominent red eyeshine, which would explain the glowing red eyes described. Owls can also make a number of odd sounds, have large heads relative to their bodies with rounded, flat faces that can appear monkey-like (seriously, go look at a picture of a monkey's face compared to an owl's), and they are decidedly clumsy on the ground. That said, size is an issue—a bird twenty inches (51 cm) tall is obviously no six-foot (2 m) monster—but even a small owl can seem intimidating and larger-than-life if it is swooping toward you in the dark, and barred owls do sport up to a five-foot (1.5 m) wingspan.

To demonstrate this concept, Nickell ran an informal size perception experiment for a 2010 episode of the Discovery Channel show *MonsterQuest* (Season 4, Episode 5), where he asked people to drive down a dark road lined with variably sized plywood Mothman figures sporting red bike reflector eyes. As expected, volunteers struggled to guess the heights correctly, with some even doubling their size, and this was under decidedly less stressful conditions than those experienced by the Scarberrys and Mallettes.

To explain why Mothman sightings continued after the initial November 15 encounter, we can look back at what we know about the psychological factors involved in hauntings. Just like heightened awareness due to fear causes people to see ghosts (which, by the way, were also reported in the area more frequently during the Mothman craze), monsters might start to appear in the shadows at the edge of their yards or while investigating a creepy, abandoned military facility. This was helped along by a number of pranksters and can also explain the other high strangeness documented at the time.

Additionally, it is telling that the sightings slowed down and stopped in the wake of the bridge collapse. Suddenly, people had bigger things to worry about than a strange creature flying around town, and when it comes to monsters and other paranormal phenomena, if it's out of mind, it's out of sight. As for the TNT area, the real scare is that in 1981 the area was designated a Superfund Site and slated for cleanup by the federal government after it was discovered that it was heavily contaminated by trinitrotoluene (TNT), its byproducts, and asbestos. Maybe Team Mutant was onto something after all . . .

THE LOCH NESS MONSTER

Whether it's the vast, unknown depths of the ocean, or the deep, cold waters of a Highland lake, large bodies of water have always been imbued with an inherent level of spookiness. Even deep water by itself is enough to scare some people, a fear that is known as thalassophobia. Loch Ness is a lake located along the Great Glen Fault, a crack between two sections of Earth's crust that cuts across the country of Scotland and formed during a cycle of mountain building known as the Caledonian Orogeny. This was during the assembly of the supercontinent Pangaea, which also created the Appalachian Mountains in North America. (Podcast listeners, you didn't think you were getting out of this book without at least a little bit of a geology lesson, did you?)

Hundreds of millions of years later, during the last Ice Age (which ended about 11,700 years ago), glaciers flowed across the landscape, carving a steep-sided valley along the Great Glen Fault. The deeper portions of this valley filled up with water to create a series of five, interconnected lakes, of which Loch Ness is the largest and deepest, at 23 miles (37 km) long and 788 feet (240 m) deep. These ancient waters are supposedly home to what is arguably the most famous cryptid in the world: the Loch Ness Monster, or Nessie for short.

Nessie in the News

The legend of the Loch Ness Monster began with three newspaper articles published in the early 1930s. The first, published in 1930, is known as the "three young anglers" sighting. A group of trout fisherman were out on a boat when something breached the water over 1,500 feet (457 m) away and began speeding toward them. When it was about six hundred feet (183 m) out, it veered off to the right and disappeared but pushed a two-and-a-half foot (1 m) wave into their boat. Not the most thrilling story—they didn't even see whatever was rushing through the water—but subsequent news pieces that referenced the anglers' experience mentioned a possible monster in Loch Ness and the seeds of the legend were sown.

The next report came three years later in 1933 from local hotel owners Aldie and John Mackay. According to a newspaper article written by their friend, a part-time journalist named Alex Campbell, the couple noticed a great disturbance about three-quarters of a mile (1 km) offshore and observed a creature with a whalelike body rolling and plunging through the water for over a minute before it disappeared.

A follow-up interview, however, revealed Campbell had taken a few liberties with their story. It was Aldie who saw an animal—John only saw splashing—and she initially mistook the disturbance for ducks fighting, which is not nearly as dramatic as what Campbell described. She also noted that she actually observed two humps in the water, not a singular whalelike creature (which skeptics point out could very well mean they just saw a couple of seals that made their way into the lake from the North Sea via the River Ness).

Overall, Campbell's story failed to make any big waves and was mostly dismissed by locals, including a local steamship captain named John MacDonald, who was insistent the Mackays merely saw a school of salmon swimming near the surface of the lake. MacDonald also took umbrage with Campbell's assertion that there had been rumors of a monster in Loch Ness for generations—he knew of no such thing.

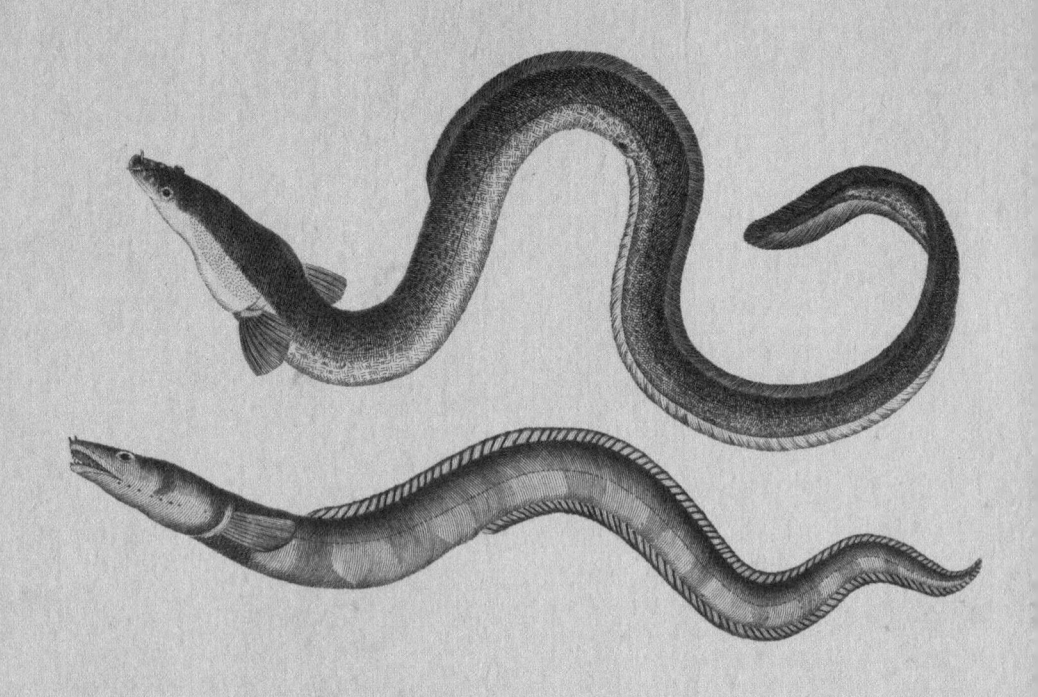

The final news story, and the one that launched Nessie onto the world stage, appeared in *The Inverness Courier* in August 1933. The newspaper published a letter from a man named George Spicer, who wrote of a creature resembling a "dragon" or a "prehistoric animal" that crossed the road in front of him and his wife while they were driving around the lake. The Spicers claimed the monster was six to eight feet (2 m) long, with gray skin and a long neck that rapidly undulated as it walked. They also noted it was carrying the body of a lamb or other animal but would later abandon that detail. Also suspicious is the fact that in later retellings, the creature grew to twenty-five to thirty feet (8–9 m) long. As William Roe's sasquatch sighting (page 108) turned bigfoot into an ape, the Spicers' story established Nessie as a prehistoric reptile with a long neck: the plesiosaur that we are all familiar with today.

MOVIE MAGIC?

There are those in the cryptozoology community who argue that Nessie was not discovered until the 1930s because the area around Loch Ness was not frequented by travelers before then. This is patently false, though. The lake was part of a busy shipping channel that ran through the Great Glen lakes after the completion of a canal system in 1822 and became a popular tourist destination for the Victorians. Either Nessie didn't enter the lake until the 1930s, or something else happened at the time, and skeptics think that something was the release of a popular movie earlier in 1933 that left the public ready to see prehistoric monsters—*King Kong*. One particular scene in that movie shows a sauropod-type dinosaur rising out of a lake, overturning a raft, and then pursuing the crew onto land. Some believe this scene bears a more-than-coincidental resemblance to the road crossing described by the Spicers. Sometimes, it's life that imitates art.

Nessie Caught on Camera?

❖◆❖

Once the Spicers' story spread, the hunt was on to capture evidence of the elusive monster that lived in Loch Ness, and new sightings started to happen with regularity. According to The Official Loch Ness Monster Sightings Register, there have been over 1,150 sightings to date. (Although this includes pre-1933 sightings that were tacked on later to flesh out the record.) Photo evidence also started to roll in. One of the first was the Nessie photo we are all familiar with, taken by Robert K. Wilson in April 1934 and often referred to as the "surgeon's photograph." The close-cropped, and more commonly seen, version of the image shows the head and neck of what appears to be a plesiosaur rising up out of the water.

Despite being the most famous image of Nessie, at least in the minds of the public, and the one that further cemented the idea that the monster of Loch Ness is a plesiosaur, it was, in all likelihood, a hoax. A man named Ian Wetherell confessed in a 1975 newspaper article that he helped his father, Marmaduke Wetherell (which is an incredible name, by the way), create the creature seen in Wilson's photo by mounting a model monster head and neck onto a toy submarine. As with Bob Heironimus' bigfoot suit confession (see page 116), we shouldn't take Wetherell's story completely on faith, but the circumstantial evidence does add up, especially the fact that Marmaduke Wetherell was involved in an earlier Nessie hoax where he was caught by the *Daily Mail* faking footprints after they commissioned him to search for the creature. And even if the Wetherell family wasn't the original source of the fakery, it becomes quite obvious when you see a less cropped version of the surgeon's photograph that the Nessie captured on film by Wilson was not a large, living, prehistoric reptile, but actually a fairly small model.

Numerous other photos and even video footage have surfaced over the years, but according to a very thorough accounting of all notable ones by paleontologist Darren Naish in his book, *Hunting Monsters: Cryptozoology and the Reality Behind the Myths*, they are all problematic in one way or another. Some are fakes, and the rest are too ambiguous to be of value as evidence or are likely misidentifications of other objects or animals. As with bigfoot, it is remarkable that the best photo evidence we have is decades old, and in this case, is almost certainly a hoax. Browsing the recent photos on the Official Sightings Register reveals image after image that is disappointingly blurry in an age of 4K cameras and that could easily be another animal or just a floating log or can clearly be chalked up to apophenia.

The Science of Nessie

◆◆◆

As far as science knows, plesiosaurs, which are a group of marine reptiles that lived alongside the dinosaurs, went extinct around sixty-five million years ago at the end of the Cretaceous period, after a massive asteroid slammed into what is now the Yucatán Peninsula. The hope of cryptozoologists and Nessie fans is that one of these species managed to survive that mass extinction (which took out over 75 percent of all species on Earth, making way for mammals) and maintain a large enough breeding population through today. It's not unheard of—scientists thought the coelacanth, a type of deep-sea fish, went extinct with the dinosaurs because they disappeared from the fossil record at the same time, but then a fisherman caught one off the coast of South Africa in 1938. However, coelacanths live at depths of around one thousand feet (304 m) in a vast ocean—easy to miss for a while, although the point should be made that we *did* still find them almost ninety years ago, without even looking for them and without any sophisticated technology.

Loch Ness, on the other hand, is a big lake, but it is obviously much smaller and shallower than the ocean and is not big enough to hide or sustain a large, carnivorous reptile. People have even done the math on how many fish are available to eat in the lake, and it would not be enough to feed a large enough breeding group to allow them to exist for any significant length of time. And just like in the case of bigfoot, no bodies, fossils, or other physical evidence for Nessie have ever been recovered; any such pieces of evidence presented have been found to be fakes or mistaken IDs. Extensive SONAR surveys also haven't produced anything conclusive (and have been tainted by hoaxes). The same goes for dredging and submarine searches of the bottom of the lake.

Moreover, geologically, it is not feasible that Nessie existed in the lake earlier than the end of the last Ice Age (ca. 11,700 years ago), because what would become Loch Ness was covered in a half-mile-thick (805 m) ice sheet. Some argue this confirms that the monster made its way up the River Ness from the Atlantic Ocean sometime more recently, but the fact remains that the lake is too cold to support a cold-blooded reptile population.

As with bigfoot and Mothman, the Loch Ness monster is another cryptid that can probably be explained by people misidentifying another animal. (Are you sensing a pattern, yet?) Other animals proposed as sources of Nessie sightings include seals, eels, salmon, otters, and even deer or elephants.

My personal favorite explanation that has been proposed to explain Nessie is that people are seeing bubbles or disturbances in the water created by geologic activity, as the lake does fall along an active fault line. And in fact, the early 1930s were at the tail end of a period of unrest along the fault, meaning there was increased earthquake activity. Ultimately, the Loch Ness monster is likely to be a mix of several of the proposed animals and natural phenomena, along with a helpful dose of wishful thinking and imagination. After all, brains are still weird.

Something Spooky

Things got exciting for us Midwestern Mothman fans when in 2011, sightings of the cryptid began happening in the Chicago, Illinois, area, over four hundred miles (644 km) away from Point Pleasant. They peaked in 2017, with a total of fifty-five sightings that year alone, and some took this to mean that Mothman is not a singular, supernatural entity, but a species of animal (for which the plural would be Mothpeople? Mothmen? Mothsman?) whose range is expanding.

In this case, we face the same issues as with bigfoot in terms of maintaining a big enough breeding population and a lack of bodies or other physical evidence. That said, misidentified sandhill cranes are actually a more feasible explanation for Mothman sightings in the Chicago area, given that Chicago falls along their natural migration path. Their long necks are still a problem (Mothman was described as having little to no neck), but coincidentally, a few days before writing this, I was driving home and saw a sandhill crane hovering above the road against a stiff wind with its wings spread wide, and I'll be damned if it didn't look Mothman-like.

Test Your Knowledge

Creeping Cryptids

How well do you know your cryptids? For each statement below, decide if you think the statement applies to a cryptid (existence is unsubstantiated by science) or a known animal (scientific proof of existence).

A. Described during the fifteenth century as a "monstrous beast, with the head of a fox, the hands of a man, the tail of a monkey, and that wonderful provision of nature, a bag in which to carry its young."

B. A carnivorous canine-looking beast with a rodent-like tail and a pouch, known for being able to open its mouth to almost a full 90 degrees.

Answers on page 201

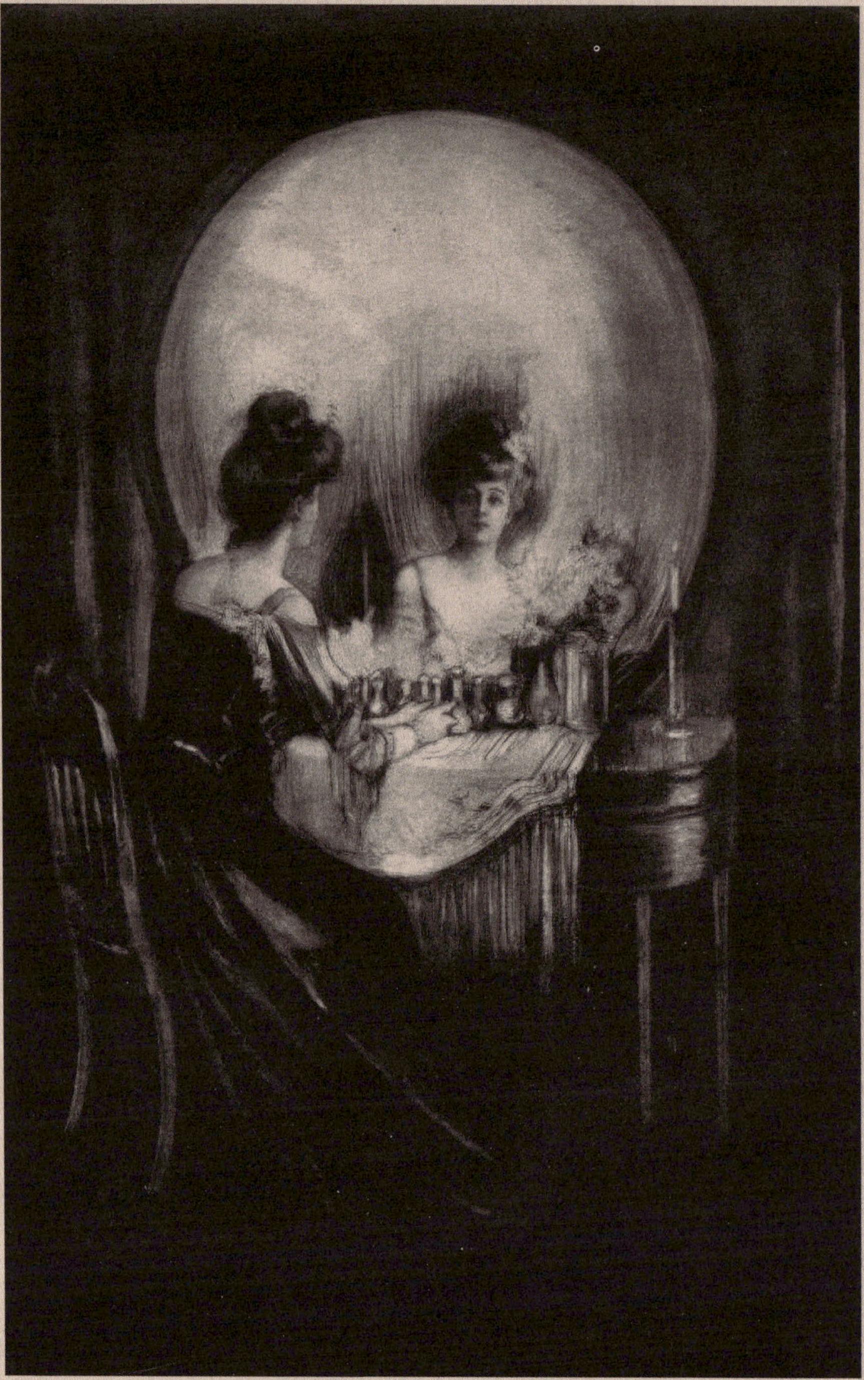

URBAN LEGENDS

Urban legends are a particular type of folklore featuring stories that are told as if they are factual but are actually fictional. They can also be exaggerated or sensationalized versions of real events. The stories are typically passed via word of mouth (or these days, on social media) and are almost always anecdotal (a "friend of a friend" is a common source). They are told in a way that encourages belief, helped along because they contain details that are adaptable to a certain region, city, or a single location, but usually seem a little too coincidental to be true. In fact, "urban legend" can also be used synonymously for "too good to be true." Urban legends are the updated version of classic monster stories, often featuring modern technology, and are a current representation of our social fears and anxieties. So, in true sleepover fashion, grab your coziest pajamas and favorite stuffed animal and meet me back here to learn about the origins of three of the spookiest ones.

BLOODY MARY

Picture this: You're ten years old. It's midnight and you're sleeping over at a friend's house with a group of other kids. You've just been dared to go into the dark bathroom, alone, with only a candle in hand. Once inside, your job is simple: Look into the mirror and speak the name "Bloody Mary" three times to see if she materializes behind you. You go in, expecting to see nothing (because it's just a silly game, right?), but as you say the words and stare into the mirror, something strange starts to happen to your reflection. Your face becomes distorted and monstrous before your very eyes. Terrified, you flip on the light switch and vacate the bathroom as quickly as possible, emerging to shrieks and giggles from your friends waiting on the other side of the door. You tell them what you saw, and while they're suspicious you're making it up, everyone agrees it's time to move on to a less macabre activity.

The scenario I just described is based on the version of the Bloody Mary urban legend ritual I learned when I was a kid. My own summoning attempts (and I don't remember doing this more than once or twice) didn't result in anything unusual beyond a case of the creeps, but as it turns out, there's actually a possible scientific explanation for why the Bloody Mary ritual sometimes gets results. Let's shine some candlelight on the history of this popular urban legend, and find out why, several years after I learned about the science behind it, I still avoid looking in the mirror at all costs if I have to get up to pee in the night.

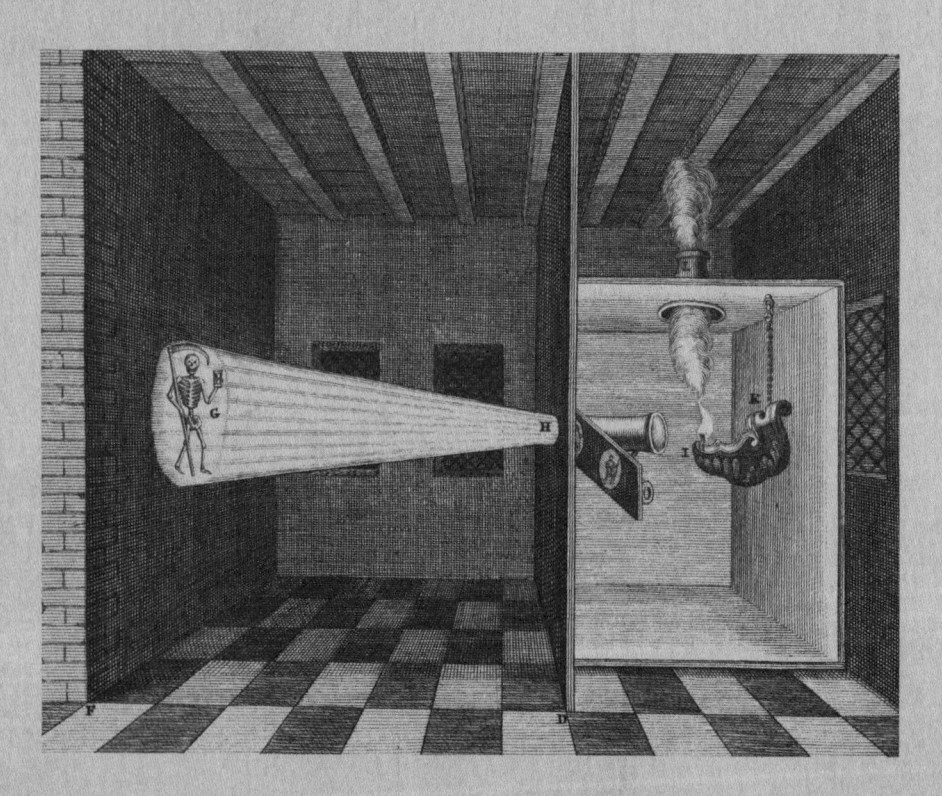

THE ORIGIN

◆◆◆

The basic setup for Bloody Mary is that one or more people must stand in front of a mirror in the dark, typically with a single light source, and speak an incantation to try to get the legendary Mary to appear. Like any good urban legend, the details of Mary's backstory, the summoning ritual, and the result of that summoning vary depending on who you ask or where you live. Here's a summary of just some of the possibilities:

- **Mary's backstory:** Mary is known by several names, including Bloody Mary, Mary Worth, Mary Whales, Hell Mary, Black Agnes, and even Kathy (which might be one of the least threatening names ever, but to each their own). In some versions of the legend, Mary was a woman who was executed for practicing witchcraft. In others, she was a young woman who died in a car accident, or a mother whose children tragically passed away. She's also been linked to real historical figures, like Mary Tudor (Queen Mary I of England), who was nicknamed Bloody Mary because she had a large number of Protestants burned for heresy.

- **Summoning rituals:** Summoning Bloody Mary can be as simple as speaking her name three or some other specified number of times. Other versions require the repetition of a phrase, such as "I believe in Mary Worth" or "Bloody Mary, I killed your baby" (rude!). Sometimes you're required to have a certain number of candles or turn around in a circle as you say her name, or even flush a toilet to complete the ritual.

- **The aftermath:** There are a wide variety of increasingly horrifying things that are said to happen if Mary appears. She might just stare at you threateningly from the mirror, reach out to scratch your eyes out, or in the extreme versions, kill you or drag you into the mirror with her.

Bloody Mary is probably derived from a divination ritual that dates back to as early as 1786, when it was mentioned in a footnote in Robert Burns's poem, "Halloween." In this original version, young women peered into a mirror while holding a candle or walked backward up the stairs while holding a hand mirror. Divination using a mirror is known as catoptromancy, and the goal in this case was for the girl to see her future husband's face in the reflection. The alternative was that the Grim Reaper or even her own corpse might appear instead, which meant that she was destined to die before she married.

This also gives us an alternative origin for the name Bloody Mary, because women participating in the early twentieth-century version would ask, "Will I be bloody, or will I be married?" And it goes to show you just how quickly things change as society advances—it was only a few decades before the publishing of Burns's poem that women in the United Kingdom were still being executed for witchcraft and in some parts of Europe, it was still happening.

There's a Ghost in My Toilet

Hanako-san, also known as Toire no Hanako or "Hanako of the Toilet," is often referred to as the Japanese Bloody Mary and is discussed among school-age children. The legend of Hanako tells the story of a young girl who haunts the stalls of public bathrooms, typically in schools. To summon Hanako you must first find her stall, typically the third stall of the third-floor bathroom, and knock three times. In most versions of the story Hanako will respond by opening the stall door slightly, reaching out a bloody hand, and pulling the summoner into the toilet. What happens next depends on the regional telling. Sometimes the toilet leads the summoner straight to hell, but in one version of the story — perhaps my favorite version — the toilet leads to a three-headed lizard that gobbles up the beckoner.

The Science

Now we can circle back to why learning about this made me afraid to look into mirrors in dark or dimly lit rooms. In general, the Bloody Mary ritual exploits similar psychological tricks to those that might lead us to see ghosts, i.e., things can get weird when our brains try to make sense of visual stimuli in dark rooms. In 2010, psychologist Giovanni Caputo put this to the test and sent fifty people into a dimly lit room to stare at their faces in a mirror for ten minutes. For most of the participants, it took *less than a minute* for their faces to become distorted, and two-thirds of them reported seeing "huge deformations" of their own faces. Significant portions of the group also saw "fantastical or monstrous beings" (48 percent!), the face of a parent or relative, a stranger, an animal's face, or an elderly woman or child. Moreover, all fifty participants said they felt a sense of unfamiliarity or "otherness" while staring into the mirror. It's easy to imagine how this effect could bring the legend of Bloody Mary to life for some people, especially when you prime them with a scary backstory.

Caputo named this newfound perceptual phenomenon "strange face illusion." The mechanism behind it may be related to another type of optical illusion known as Troxler fading, which occurs when you stare at the same, unchanging point for a long time. The longer you look, and in the absence of new visual stimuli, the more your brain starts to filter out what it considers nonessential information, and the image around that fixed point starts to appear blurry, faded, or distorted. The purpose of this and similar perceptual phenomena is to avoid overloading you and allow you to focus only on what's important.

One of my favorite nonvisual examples of the brain's sensory-filtering powers is that you probably can't feel your underwear right now (and if you can, please buy new underwear). You certainly felt the fabric slide into place this morning, but since then, your brain has been filtering out that stimuli, which is great, because who wants to spend their whole day distracted by their underwear? As we saw with ghosts though, the flip side to your brain's amazing ability to process and filter information is that sometimes things can get a bit confused. And in the case of Bloody Mary, as your brain struggles to interpret what it sees in a dimly lit room and tries to fill in the gaps, something as normal as your own face might become a monster. All I know is I'm not trying to find out what I might see in my bathroom mirror in the middle of the night.

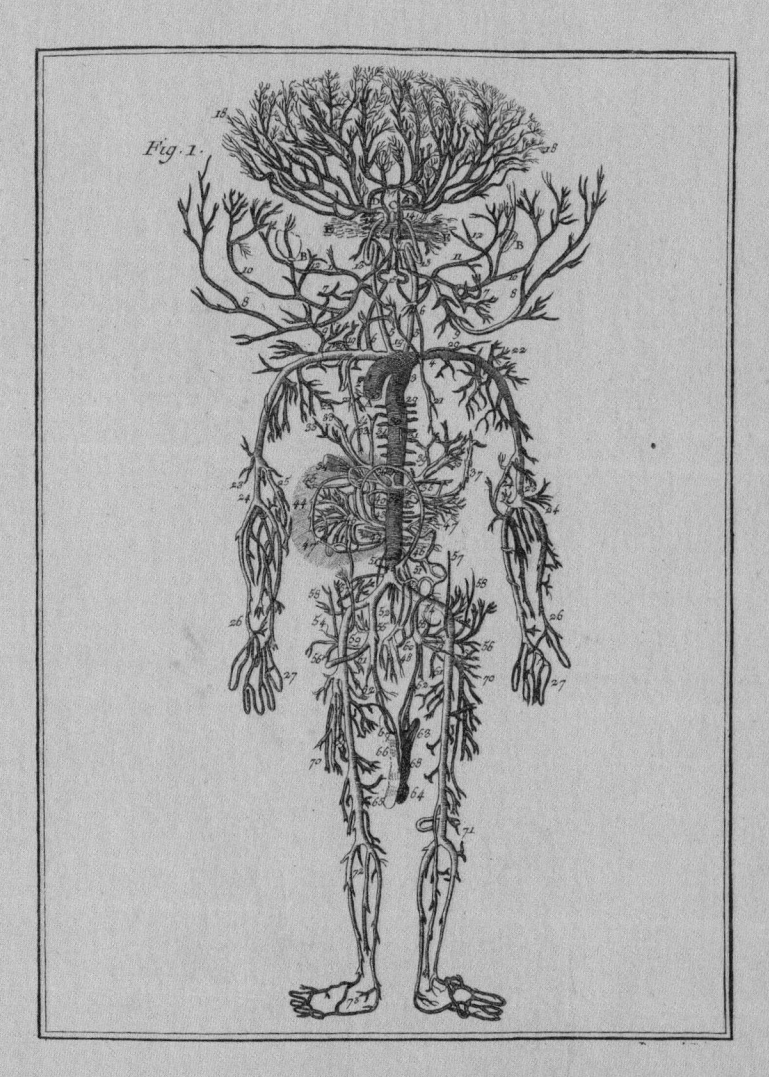

BLACK-EYED CHILDREN

Now imagine it's late at night (isn't it always in these things?), you're home alone, and you hear a knock at your front door. You normally wouldn't answer it this late (or ever, if you're me), but you peek out the window and notice there are two young children standing on your porch, so you feel obligated to find out if they need help. Upon opening the door, you notice that they're wearing outdated clothing but otherwise seem like normal kids. Things start to get weird after you start talking to them—they speak in odd, monotone voices, and begin asking, and then insisting, that you let them into the house. As you continue to look at the children, you notice that their eyes are very dark—in fact, do they have any whites to their eyes at all? You are overcome with a feeling of dread and are absolutely not letting these kids inside your house, but you still feel enough of a sense of obligation to call the police on their behalf to get them whatever help they need. You close the door, and it takes you just a few seconds to grab your phone, but by the time you return, they've vanished, seemingly into thin air. Were some local kids messing with you, or did you just have an encounter with a paranormal entity?

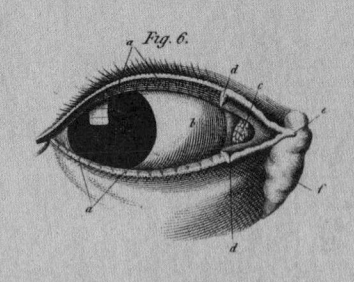

The story above is a typical encounter with the black-eyed children (also known as black-eyed kids or BEKs), an urban legend that started in a Usenet newsgroup (an early version of an internet forum or message board) in 1997, and quickly took off, with new encounters appearing elsewhere online and seeping into paranormal media and literature. These creepy kids have been called ghosts, demons, vampires, and even extraterrestrials, so let's turn our (totally normal, not black) eyes toward where they originated.

The Origin

The original black-eyed children encounter was shared in 1997 by a man named Brian Bethel of Abilene, Texas, United States. He reported that while he was in his car in a movie theater parking lot, he heard a knock on his window and looked up to see a pair of boys, aged around ten to fourteen years old, staring at him. He opened his window to talk to them, and the boys began trying to convince him to drive them to their house. Bethel found the way they spoke and their mannerisms unsettling, and eventually he noticed their completely black eyes with no pupil, iris, or sclera visible. The boys noticed Bethel's fear and became very upset, shouting that they couldn't come into the car without being invited and that he needed to *LET. THEM. IN!* At this point, Bethel sped out of the parking lot, keeping the boys in his peripheral vision, but when he turned his head to take one last full glance, they had disappeared.

Bethel's (somewhat rambling) story immediately rings false in a world where creepypastas (internet speak for widely shared—copied and pasted—spooky stories) abound. I've certainly read much more convincing tales on the likes of Reddit's r/NoSleep page, where the goal is to post scary, fictional stories as if they are real. Additionally, according to some sleuthing by Brian Dunning of the *Skeptoid* podcast, the same day Bethel shared his BEK encounter story to Usenet, he also wrote another post musing on being able to manifest an entity like Bloody Mary into existence through "collective force of will." Basically, all signs point to Bethel making it up, although we should note that he has spoken to many news outlets and maintained the veracity of his story. And while it's been claimed that BEKs show up in stories dating back as far as the 1950s, the older stories are all anecdotal and, like with cryptids, seem to have been tacked on retroactively in the hopes of adding credibility with the appearance of a long-lived history.

As is required of an urban legend, encounters with BEKs follow the same general pattern with some changeable details. For example, black-eyed kids can be in groups or alone and range in age from six to sixteen years old. They might be found hitchhiking or panhandling or approaching random cars or houses asking to be let inside. Similar to vampire folklore, BEKs must be invited inside a home or vehicle—they cannot enter on their own—and some report feeling compelled to give in to their requests as if the kids were exerting some psychic power. (Bethel mentions his hand unconsciously drifting toward the door handle at one point, too.)

An odd detail that is included in many stories is that the person immediately goes to the door with a weapon, commonly a firearm, or retrieves one shortly into the encounter, you know, like you do when you're talking to kids you don't know who tell you they need help. The funny thing is that no one really ever seems to know what happens after you let them into your house or car, but I suppose the believer's argument would be that those poor souls aren't around to share their story with the internet.

THE SCIENCE

Because the Black-Eyed Children urban legend is based on an internet forum post, it's safe to assume that all the encounters are made up for internet clout, and there's also no hard evidence for them in the form of photos or videos. There are some versions of the story in which people claim they got video footage of an encounter, but it was too scary, so they immediately deleted it (suuuuuure . . .).

If we accept that some of them are representative of real-world events, though, there are a few hypotheses we can make about what people are actually seeing. One of the common skeptical solutions invoked is that BEK encounters are just hoaxes using special contact lenses that cover the entire iris and sclera (the white of the eye) in black. These are quite expensive, though, and are reportedly very uncomfortable, making them an unlikely choice for children to be able to access or for their parents to force them to wear in the name of a prank.

Some have also suggested the children are under the influence of some drug that caused their pupils to dilate and could perhaps also explain their strange behavior. With the advent of video doorbells, however, you'd think that in either of these possibilities, someone would have managed to get one of these creepy kids on camera at some point.

My own hypothesis to explain BEK encounters is that in some cases, people are experiencing the strange face illusion. In a follow-up study on facial perception by Giovanni Caputo, he asked pairs of people to stare at each other in a dimly lit room for ten minutes. Within a minute, participants began to see distortions, sometimes monstrous, of their respective partners' faces. Sometimes, they felt as if they were outside of their own bodies or that time was slowing and stretching. For BEK encounters that happen in the evenings or low lighting, this seems like it could explain why it often takes a little while for people to realize the children's eyes look black — there needs to be enough time for the strange face illusion to kick in — and why most experiencers note they felt very uneasy or afraid. The appearance of black eyes could be exacerbated by the fact that people's pupils are dilated in the dark. Of course, my solution supposes people are scaring themselves enough to ignore the real requests of children asking for help, so better to hope that BEK stories are just invented to scare others on the internet, which, in all likelihood, is the real explanation.

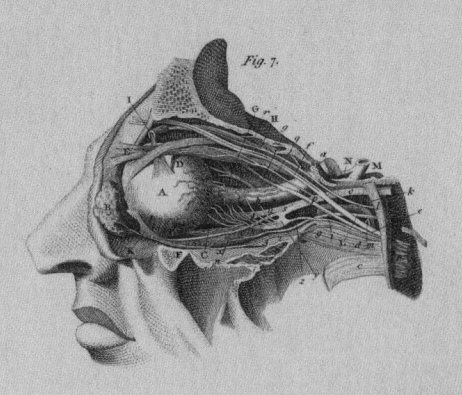

BERMUDA TRIANGLE

It was December 5, 1945, and five bombers headed out on a training flight from the naval base in Fort Lauderdale, Florida, United States, under the command of Lieutenant Charles C. Taylor, an experienced naval aviator with multiple World War II combat tours under his belt. The flight plan for what was called Flight 19 was meant to be a test of the crew's navigational skills. It called for them to head east to drop a series of practice bombs over an area called the Hen and Chickens Shoals and then fly over Grand Bahama Island before finally heading back to Fort Lauderdale. They made their bombing run successfully, but then things started to go horribly wrong.

Almost two hours into the flight, Lt. Taylor was heard on the radio saying that he wasn't sure where they were and that both of his compasses were out. He was certain they must be somewhere over the Florida Keys, but nothing he was seeing made sense. Radio transmissions continued to come in, revealing that after heading north for a while, the group of planes began changing directions, desperately trying to find land. It took close to two hours more for Navy personnel to finally locate Flight 19 using previous radio transmissions, and they were not anywhere near the Florida Keys. They were actually off the east coast of central Florida, between two hundred to four hundred miles (322–644 km) north of the Bahamas. If they had just flown west, they would have reached land, but for unknown reasons, this information wasn't transmitted to Flight 19—perhaps it was assumed they couldn't be reached because of the distance or interference. Dusk fell, storms moved into the area, and fuel was getting low. Knowing this, two additional planes were dispatched to begin the search and hopefully recover the crew alive. One of those rescue planes, along with all five Flight 19 aircraft, and both of their crews (a total of twenty-seven men), were never seen again.

In the 1950s, articles began popping up that included Flight 19 as just one of several seemingly mysterious disappearances of planes and ships that had occurred in the area that we now call the Bermuda Triangle, and a new urban legend was born. But, as these things usually go, things aren't quite as mysterious or sinister as they seem.

The Legend Grows

Today, the Bermuda Triangle (also known as the Devil's Triangle) is defined as a triangular-shaped area of the Atlantic Ocean that falls between Florida, Bermuda, and Puerto Rico, covering an area of around five hundred thousand square miles (1.3 million km^2). The name comes from a 1964 pulp magazine article called "The Deadly Bermuda Triangle" written by Vincent Gaddis (and if you're like me and unfamiliar with pulp magazines, they are inexpensive magazines full of typically *fictional* stories that were printed on cheap wood pulp paper). Like in the earlier news stories, Gaddis compiled stories of shipwrecks and plane crashes from the area, added some embellishments to make them seem more mysterious (like you do with any good urban legend), and primed everyone to start attributing any shipwreck or plane crash in that area to an otherworldly force at work. Since then, many writers have elaborated on Gaddis's stories. A book by Charles Berlitz published in 1974 called *The Bermuda Triangle* was particularly popular and cemented the Triangle's paranormal association, offering various explanations for the activity there, including extraterrestrials, time slips, or even an underwater civilization.

Just Another Triangle

The Bermuda Triangle is by far the most famous paranormal triangle but the thing about triangles is that you can find them just about anywhere. So, it should come as no surprise that there are almost a dozen triangles around the world that have been deemed paranormal.

The Bridgewater Triangle, named in 1983 by cryptozoologist Loren Coleman, is one of the few well-known land triangles. The area of the triangle covers two hundred square miles (518 km²) of land in southeast Massachusetts, United States, and is considered one of the most highly concentrated areas for paranormal activity. Think of something strange or supernatural, and I can just about guarantee somebody has claimed to see, hear, or smell that thing within the Bridgewater Triangle. That being said, the reports are all so wildly different from one another that you could connect any three points on a map and sort all of the weird reports and sightings from that area over its recorded history, and I am willing to bet you'll find a similar pattern.

DEMYSTIFYING FLIGHT 19

◆◆◆

Through all the legend-building, Flight 19 continued to be a seminal example of the strange forces at work in the Bermuda Triangle, with paranormal enthusiasts latching on to the seemingly strange details like the malfunctioning compasses, the loss of the search plane, and the lack of recovery of any wreckage or bodies. However, thanks to an extensive analysis of the events of Flight 19 by former pilot and librarian, Larry Kusche, author of the 1975 book *The Bermuda Triangle Mystery: Solved* and the 1980 book *The Disappearance of Flight 19*, we can see that the disappearance of Flight 19, while a tragic accident, was actually the result of nothing but human error. Take the three "spooky" details I noted above:

> • **Malfunctioning compasses:** Bermuda Triangle believers point out that both compasses malfunctioning at the same time would be an incredibly rare, if not impossible, event and often suggest there is some magnetic anomaly or other mysterious force affecting them in that area.
>
> In reality, the Flight 19 compasses were not malfunctioning, they just disagreed with where Lt. Taylor believed he was. He had likely gotten turned around after the bombing practice exercise and mistook some of the small islands near the Bahamas for the Florida Keys. Once his mind seized on that interpretation, he staunchly refused to fly west, thinking he would just end up in the Gulf of Mexico, and continued to push north along the east coast of Florida. Radio calls between the planes reveal some crew members disagreed with this plan and wanted to try heading west, but they had no choice but to listen to their leader.
>
> • **Loss of the search plane:** The search plane that disappeared was a Martin PBM Mariner. These planes were nicknamed "flying

gas tanks" because they were designed for long-distance patrols and had to carry a large amount of fuel. I'm sure you can already guess where this is going, but a ship in the area reported seeing a huge fireball streak across the sky and then passing through an oil slick on the surface of the water in the vicinity of where the Martin Mariner was flying that night, suggesting the plane exploded.

Unsurprisingly, this detail is often missing from sensationalized, urban legend–style retellings of the events, and while it is a heck of a coincidence, that doesn't mean it was paranormal. Additionally, the day after the disappearance of Flight 19, over two hundred planes and seventeen ships went out despite the poor weather and heavy seas to continue the search. And guess what? They all made it back.

• **Lack of wreckage or bodies:** In general, the ocean is much larger and deeper than people realize—it took over seventy years for the *Titanic*, a much bigger vessel than a plane, to be found, and searchers knew its exact location when it sank. Malaysia Airlines Flight 370, which crashed into the Indian Ocean in 2014, a time when we had access to much more advanced navigation and search technology, has never been found beyond a few pieces of wreckage that have washed up in the years since.

The real spookiest fact about the Bermuda Triangle is probably that the deepest point in the Atlantic Ocean, called the Milwaukee Depth, is located within it. It's there that a part of the Puerto Rico Trench reaches a depth of 27,493 feet (8,380 m), which is deep enough to fit all but about 1,500 feet (457 m) of the height of Mount Everest.

The Science: Other Ocean Oddities

In-depth analyses of other famous Bermuda Triangle incidents by Kusche and others reveal similarly logical explanations for "mysterious" accidents or disappearances, rampant exaggerations of facts and figures in many retellings, and some stories that were outright fabrications. Additional factors that have been suggested to explain incidents include:

- **Stormy weather:** There are a large number of tropical storms, including hurricanes, that pass through the area, so safe to say, the weather can get rough. These types of storms can also generate unpredictable weather phenomena like waterspouts and powerful downdrafts that might catch aircraft or boats off guard. Many stories say that a plane or ship disappeared when the weather was completely calm, but Larry Kusche's analysis showed that the meteorological records often tell a different story.

- **Aircraft instrumentation failures:** Precipitation static is a buildup of static electricity on the exterior shell of an airplane when it flies through rain, snow, ice, or dust. Unless it is discharged, it can cause a number of problems, such as inaccurate magnetic compass readings and the loss of or interference with communication and navigation systems. Planes built after the late 1940s are equipped with static wicks to discharge any static buildup, but this could certainly have been an issue in some of the earlier Bermuda Triangle plane incidents.

- **Rogue waves:** There's a very specific height requirement for a wave to be officially considered a "rogue," but generally, they are waves that are unusually large relative to those around them — roughly double the size. Rogue waves can occur anywhere in the open ocean, so it is possible one might explain the sudden disappearance of a water vessel in the Bermuda Triangle.

• **Ocean farts:** The burial of decomposing organic matter on the ocean floor and high pressures at depth can result in a buildup of an icelike substance composed of methane gas and water known as methane hydrate. A disturbance of the ocean floor, perhaps by something like an earthquake (which does occur along the Puerto Rico Trench), might cause chunks of methane hydrate to break off and rise toward the surface. As they depressurize, a gust of methane gas bubbles would form, which could burst up at the surface quite dramatically.

It's been proposed that they might even do so with enough force to tip over a ship, which led Russian scientists studying methane craters in melting permafrost to suggest they could explain some of the more mysterious Bermuda Triangle disappearances, particularly the ones that actually happened on otherwise calm days. Others say this idea is a bit too far-fetched, though, and would definitely not be an issue for modern ships.

More generally, statistical analyses show that the number of shipwrecks and airplane incidents are no higher in the Bermuda Triangle than in other parts of the Atlantic Ocean. A report commissioned by the World Wildlife Fund in 2013 identified the most dangerous waters for shipping, and the Bermuda Triangle didn't even make the list, although it is located within one of the busiest shipping and travel corridors in the world. Despite the evidence that shipwrecks and plane crashes happen there no more frequently or mysteriously than elsewhere in the world, though, the Triangle is still considered a hotspot for paranormal or other strange activity by many.

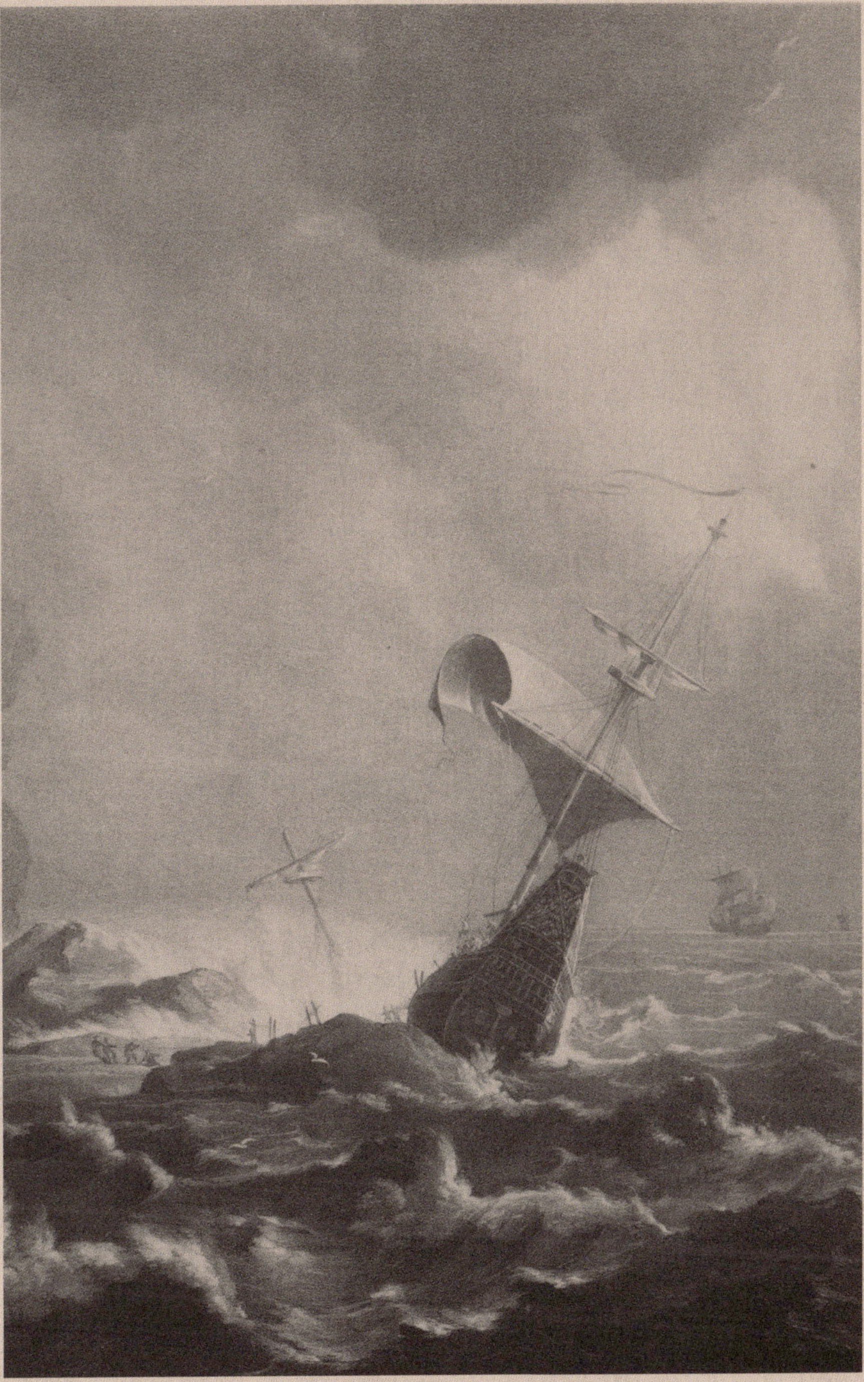

Something Spooky

Gibbs Bridge is a bridge in the middle of nowhere Ohio, United States, on a short country road. As a teenager, I had heard numerous stories about the bridge, including unexpected deaths, suicides, and ghost sightings.

A group of high-school friends and I decided it was time to learn what all the fuss was about , but after a short visit we left, underwhelmed by our Gibbs Bridge experience.

As soon as we started to leave, a car pulled out behind us. We hurried down the road and turned away from Gibbs Bridge, but the car followed close behind. Only after the lights on the car behind us turned did it occur to us that we weren't being followed by a scary homeowner or something paranormal. We were being followed by the local police. When the officer pulled us over (for going twenty over the posted speed limit), he verified we were okay and let us off with a warning. But before we pulled away, he warned us that there was some truth to the Gibbs Bridge legend and urged us to stay away.

TEST YOUR KNOWLEDGE

EERIE URBAN LEGENDS

BELOW YOU WILL FIND TWO SHORT DESCRIPTIONS OF URBAN LEGENDS OR LEGENDARY PLACES. CAN YOU GUESS WHICH ONES?

A. A group of ten experienced hikers left for a sixteen-day expedition in the Ural Mountains of Russia (then the Soviet Union) during the winter of 1959. Nine of them did not return. Almost a full month after their departure, a search party located their tent at the base of Kholat Syakhl (which translates to "dead mountain"), and nine of the hikers were found dead. Five were found near the tent. The other four bodies, located a mile and a half (2 km) from the tent, took over two months to find. Some were found with skull fractures or chest fractures, and one was missing their eyes and tongue. The official (initial) investigation concluded that the hikers succumbed to an "unknown compelling [natural] force."

B. A dark figure known to wear a flat brimmed hat, typically seen in the middle of the night near the bed of his "summoners." This internet urban legend regained popularity in 2020 when TikTok users, primarily teenagers, made videos describing him and encouraging the use of Benadryl as a way to more reliably summon the creature. This series of videos was more widely known as the Benadryl Challenge.

Answers on page 202

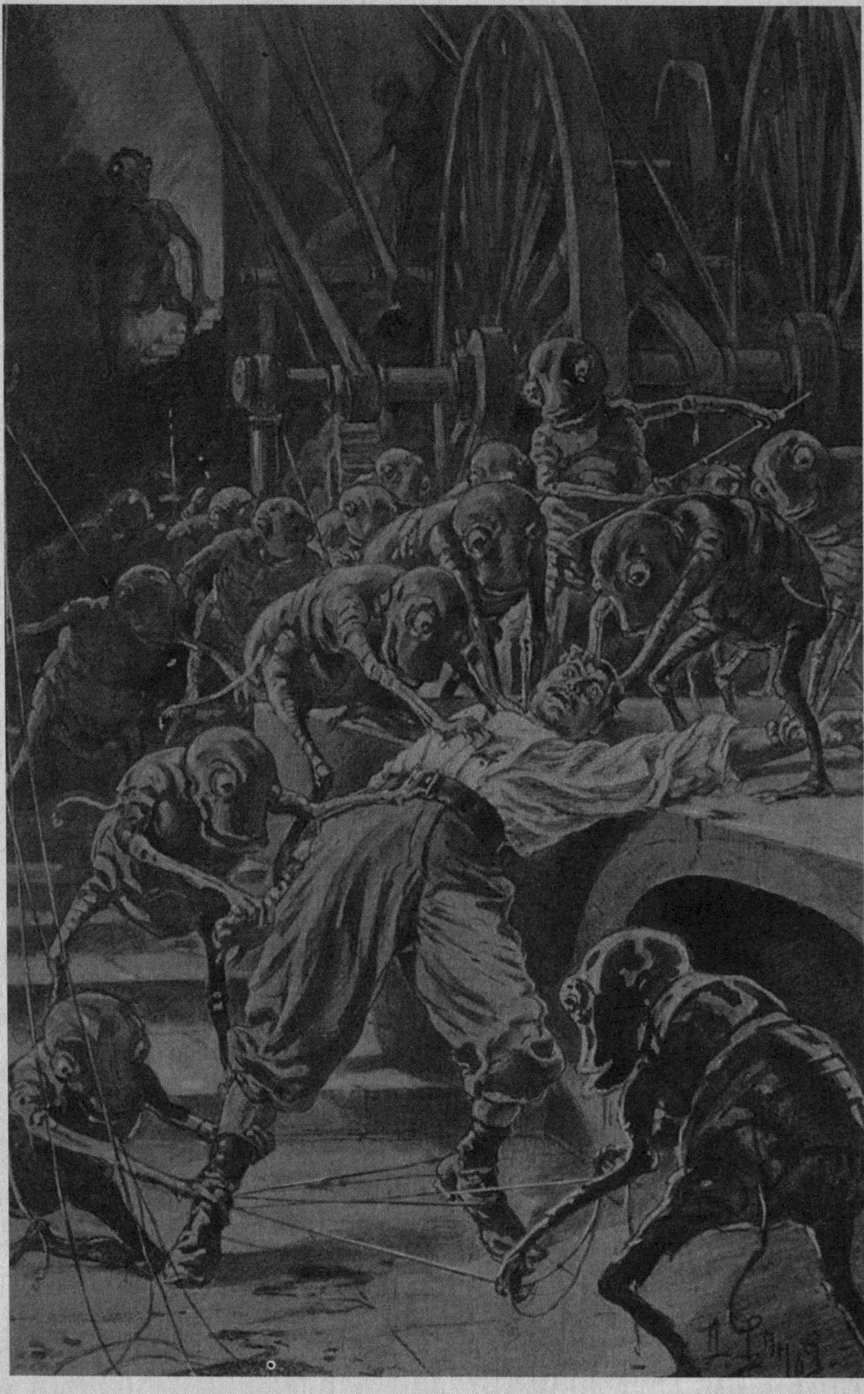

ALIENS

Throughout this book, we've seen that folklore and the paranormal have long helped humanity cope with big fears, like the inevitability of death and the monstrous capabilities of our fellow man. Thousands of years ago, when ancient scholars started to look to the sky and consider our place in the universe, the possibility of life on other planets immediately became a concern. Greek philosopher Epicurus and his disciples may have been skeptical about the existence of ghosts (see page 24), but they did believe that in an infinite universe there must be other worlds like ours, including ones with life.

Flash forward to the early- to mid-twentieth century, and the question became not so much "Are there aliens?" but "Where are the aliens?" At that time, technological innovations were happening faster than ever. With the invention of air travel, we suddenly weren't confined to Earth's surface, and by the end of World War II, we had access to unprecedented power in the form of nuclear weapons. By the time the space race kicked off in the mid-1950s, alien visitors were showing up regularly in popular science fiction, and people, who were looking to the sky more than ever, started to see some weird things.

Recent polls indicate that 75 percent of Americans believe there is life in some form elsewhere in the universe, and 49 percent believe it exists in a form similar to us. As far as alien visitors go, 41 percent believe some unidentified flying objects (UFOs) are extraterrestrial in origin. In this chapter, we'll review the history and science behind three major phenomena associated with the idea that aliens might be visiting Earth: UFOs, alien abductions, and crop circles.

ARE ALIENS EVEN PARANORMAL?

Some of you might be wondering why we've included aliens in a book otherwise aimed at examining the science behind paranormal phenomena. After all, the idea of aliens, meaning life that exists on other planets, is decidedly not paranormal. That even extends to intelligent life once we enter interstellar space and then move beyond our own galaxy, because in an infinite universe, it seems incredibly self-centered to believe that we are completely unique. In fact, there are entire branches of science and many ongoing scientific studies aimed at finding or contacting extraterrestrial life in distant star systems. As soon as we start talking about UFOs, ufology (the study of UFOs), and associated phenomena like crop circles and alien abductions, however, the water gets murky.

As it currently stands, the idea that extraterrestrials are visiting Earth (or have in the past), is very much based on pseudoscience, and many would unequivocally label it a paranormal belief. That's because, like with the existence of ghosts, the body of evidence for alien visitors is anecdotal, ambiguous (again with the blurry photos or video footage), anomalous (not repeatable!), or attributable to known natural phenomena or something man-made.

However, with the excitement in recent years about renewed UFO tracking programs within the Department of Defense (see "UAPs Are the New UFOs" on page 171), and even NASA getting involved in 2022, it feels like new inroads are being made between the scientific community and ufologists. In the end, if the goal is to find conclusive evidence of extraterrestrial life, both sides are on the same team, but we all need to agree to do it in a scientific way.

UNIDENTIFIED FLYING OBJECTS

Before we jump into UFOs, I need you to repeat after me: Unidentified does not equal aliens. Unidentified does *not* equal aliens! Unidentified DOES. NOT. EQUAL. ALIENS!

OK, I'm glad we got that off our chests.

I stress this point up front because since the first "official" UFOs were spotted in the 1940s, a popular explanation has been that they are extraterrestrial spacecrafts. This is commonly referred to as the extraterrestrial hypothesis (ETH), a shorthand that I'll use from here on out. And one of the biggest issues for skeptics when it comes to the UFO phenomena is that it is a huge leap to go from "I don't know what this is" to "It's aliens" based on the examples and data we have on hand right now.

But, as we've seen throughout this book, we humans have a knack for filling in what we can't explain with the sensational while we wait for science to catch up. With that in mind, let's grab our tinfoil hats (I'm sorry, I couldn't resist) and take a look at the history of UFOs, their (unlikely) association with extraterrestrial life, and what skeptics and science have to say about them.

Flying Saucer Mania

◆◆◆

The story of modern UFOs began on June 24, 1947, near Mineral, Washington, United States. Amateur pilot Kenneth Arnold was out in his small plane on a search mission, helping to look for a Marine Corps transport plane believed to have crashed in the area. He didn't find the missing plane, but whatever he did see that day would change the course of history.

As Arnold flew, he noticed a strange blue flash of light that he quickly traced to a chain of nine, shiny objects tearing across the sky at speeds of at least 1,200 miles per hour (1,931 kph), a speed he estimated based on how long it took them to traverse the distance between Mount Adams and Mount Rainier. (Volcanoes *and* UFOs? This guy was living the dream.) Importantly, these objects were much faster than any aircraft at that time, and they were clearly different in appearance and behavior compared to a nearby plane he could also see. Arnold guessed that each one was at least fifty feet (15 m) wide, highly reflective, and was flying at an altitude of about ten thousand feet (3,048 m), sometimes with a weaving or undulating motion.

The next day, feeling a sense of obligation given rising tensions with the Soviets (the Cold War had just kicked off that March), Arnold shared his sighting with a local newspaper, the *East Oregonian*, and they published a story with the headline "Impossible! Maybe, But Seein' Is Believin', Says Flyer." The Associated Press quickly picked up the tale, and Arnold's out-of-this-world experience became a national sensation. Within weeks of Arnold's report being published, there were hundreds of reports coming in of round, flying saucer–like crafts showing up across the United States.

Except Kenneth Arnold didn't see "flying saucers" at all.

The original news story published by the *East Oregonian* reports that Arnold described the aircrafts he saw as "saucer-like," but Arnold himself said that was a misquote. He later claimed he actually said they moved like "a saucer if you skip it across the water," and the objects he saw were crescent- or "somewhat bat-" shaped. When the story was picked up by the Associated Press, "saucer-like" became "flying saucers," and the damage was done—in the mind of the American public and the rest of the world, flying saucers were what Arnold spotted in the sky that fateful June day, so that's what everyone else saw, too.

Obviously, Arnold's contradiction is a huge problem for ufologists, as it largely invalidates the subsequent sightings. Some have tried to argue that Arnold did describe what he saw as saucers or disks, but that he later walked it back due to his discomfort about the notoriety he gained as the originator of the flying saucer phenomena. However, that reads to me as a case of trying to have your cake and eat it too, because to claim that Arnold later started lying about what he witnessed calls into question his reliability from the start. As for what he really saw, no one will ever know for sure, but possible non-alien explanations include a nearby flock of pelicans that he mistook for fast-moving objects much farther away, pieces of a meteor that broke apart in Earth's atmosphere, or a type of mirage known as a Fata Morgana.

The Government Gets Involved

By the end of 1947, over eight hundred UFO reports had been recorded from all over the United States and Canada, and it was then that the United States Air Force decided to officially investigate to rule out any national security concerns through three main projects:

1. **Project Sign:** The first investigation commenced in January 1948, and over the next year, those involved evaluated 243 UFO sightings. In a report released in early 1949, it was stated that while most of the sightings could be attributed to ordinary causes, they couldn't

conclusively rule out the possibility that people were seeing some type of advanced aircraft.

An extraterrestrial origin was also unable to be definitively ruled out, but was at least noted to be highly unlikely, and they reasonably qualified that every other possibility would have to be ruled out before that option would be considered in more depth. It was recommended that investigations continue in the interest of national security.

2. **Project Grudge:** The primary purpose of Grudge, however, was not so much to investigate, but to quell public fears about the continued UFO sightings out of concern that fear could be weaponized against United States citizens by foreign adversaries.

A few short months later, in August 1949, Project Grudge released a report that concluded UFOs were largely a product of people's minds, hoaxes, or misidentifications of known objects (man-made or natural). They also attempted to shut down any notion that UFOs were advanced, foreign (or alien) technology and declared that they posed no threat to national security.

In response to the report, the Air Force embarked on a public relations campaign to debunk UFO reports, with the goal of making them seem as unremarkable as possible, which *definitely* didn't make anyone in the general public suspicious *at all*. (That's sarcasm, in case you missed it.) Moreover, of the 244 sightings Project Grudge examined, there were still about 20 percent that they had no definitive answer for.

3. **Project Blue Book:** The most well-known of these early UFO investigations, Project Blue Book was initiated in 1952 due to a new wave of sightings and continued concerns about the Cold War and the Korean War. Project Blue Book wouldn't be disbanded until late

1969, and in the over seventeen years of its existence, the team examined 12,618 UFO reports stretching back to the originals in 1947.

Of those, 701 (about 6 percent) remained unexplained, either due to insufficient evidence or because they truly couldn't figure them out, but they concluded they posed no risk to national security, did not represent technology beyond what was possible at the time of the reports, and were not extraterrestrial in origin.

SECRETS, SUSPICIONS, AND SCIENCE

In some ways, Projects Sign, Grudge, and Blue Book probably did more harm than good in terms of bringing the public together on the issue of UFOs. People felt brushed off or even insulted by some of the conventional explanations that were offered.

Some of the criticism was internal; J. Allen Hynek, an astronomer and lead scientific consultant for the three projects, grew disenchanted with what he saw as the "debunk now, ask questions never" narrative he felt he was being forced to uphold. He believed that while it was true that most reports were explainable, the phenomenon still merited more careful scientific investigation and would go on to form the Center for UFO Studies (CUFOS).

Public suspicion also rose when it was revealed in declassified documents released in 1975 that the CIA hosted a secret panel on UFOs in 1953, known as the Robertson Panel. That panel went on to suggest that the government should publicly reject all UFO sightings without question and even monitor domestic UFO groups to make sure there were no hints of a foreign threat (. . . yikes).

Long story short, to the burgeoning ufology community, it seemed more and more likely that the government was trying to sweep UFOs under the rug because it had something to hide—and, based on the Robertson Panel, was maybe even trying to silence UFO groups. If we look at things from the perspective of government officials, these investigations accomplished exactly what they were meant to: assess national security threats. After collecting and evaluating over twelve thousand UFO reports (even if they were a bit hasty to dismiss them at times), you can't really blame them for deciding to close the books when no credible threat manifested in over twenty years of sightings.

And to their credit, in 1966, the Air Force did commission an independent inquiry into the Project Blue Book cases to determine if there was anything of scientific value to be gained—for example, evidence of extraterrestrial visitation or advanced technology. This science-based appraisal was led by nuclear physicist Edward Condon and spent two years examining a subset of the Blue Book encounters. Afterward, Condon and his team released a report that stated they saw no evidence for anything unusual or that merited further study, an honestly unsurprising result considering the vast majority of cases came down to eyewitness reports and questionable or incomplete data. The Condon Report, which was endorsed by the National Academy of Sciences, would go on to become the de facto position for scientists on the UFO phenomena, and was a major factor in Project Blue Book shutting down in 1969. The government, at least for a time, was seemingly out of the business of UFOs.

The Roswell Balloon Bonanza

◆◆◆

Another complicating factor that fostered distrust in the United States government's inquiries into UFOs was that sometimes they had their own technology to conceal in the interest of national security, and nowhere did this play out more spectacularly than in Roswell, New Mexico, United States. On June 14, 1947, a sheep rancher named W.W. ("Mac") Brazel came across some unusual debris in a field that consisted of tinfoil, "tough" paper, wooden sticks, strips of rubber, and tape with some simple designs on it. (Yes, that's really all he found in case you were expecting something a bit more exciting.) The ranch was located in a remote area about seventy-five miles (121 km) north of Roswell, so Brazel initially missed the news about Kenneth Arnold's UFO sighting just ten days later and the subsequent media craze. After he found out about it in early July, though, Brazel collected some of the debris and took it to the local sheriff, who in turn contacted the Roswell Army Air Field (RAAF, known today as Walker Air Force Base). The commander of the RAAF sent Major Jesse Marcel from the base's intelligence office to check things out.

On July 8, Marcel went to the ranch with Brazel and the sheriff to collect the remaining debris, and then, in a stunning turn of events, decided to hold a press conference that same day where he announced that the RAAF recovered one of the flying disks everyone was so excited about. The local afternoon paper, the *Roswell Daily Record*, immediately published the story, but the excitement about Marcel's announcement was to be short-lived. Within twenty-four hours, the *Daily Record*'s sister publication, the *Roswell Morning Dispatch*, published an update that the army had already debunked the "flying disk" as a weather balloon equipped with a radar target (the likely source of the sticks, foiled paper, and tape Brazel found).

For a while, that was that—people accepted the balloon explanation and moved on with their lives. That is, until a ufologist by the name of Stanton Friedman ran into Marcel in 1978, and Marcel told him a very different story from what had been publicized thirty years earlier. According to Marcel, the events at Roswell were actually a cover-up of a crashed alien ship, and the materials in the published photographs were actually fake. Friedman and Marcel took this new conspiracy theory public, and the Roswell incident took on a life of its own. Soon there were stories popping up of multiple UFO crashes across New Mexico and about bodies of dead (or sometimes living) aliens that were sent to secret government labs, but, of course, all this information came from (often secondhand) eyewitness accounts collected over thirty years after these events had supposedly occurred.

The Roswell incident became such a sensation that the Air Force was compelled to release their own response to the outlandish claims piling up. In two reports, published in 1995 and 1997, they revealed that the debris discovered by Brazel wasn't just a weather balloon, but was part of a sophisticated, high-altitude balloon apparatus equipped with experimental sensors designed to detect Soviet nuclear detonations. These spy balloons were associated with a top-secret program known as Project Mogul, which was granted a priority level of 1A, the same as that given to the Manhattan Project, the program that developed the atomic bomb during World War II. Simply put, there was a cover-up of sorts that had taken place, but in the name of national security, not because of aliens.

Importantly, the Project Mogul equipment would have looked significantly different than a standard weather balloon, which may inform why Jesse Marcel ultimately felt there was something off about that explanation. Additionally, inquiries into Marcel's military record and character by journalist and skeptic Kal K. Korff for his book on the Roswell incident revealed that Marcel had a penchant for exaggerations and mistruths. But, for many in the ufology community who already distrusted the government to tell the truth about UFOs, the Air Force's admissions about Project Mogul were too little, too late, and many took them as just more evidence of the government's untruthfulness.

UAPS ARE THE NEW UFOS

After Project Blue Book was shuttered in 1969, a few prominent UFO sightings occurred, and the Roswell conspiracy was born, but overall, at least in the eyes of the public, there wasn't much excitement through the turn of the century. That all changed on December 16, 2017, when *The New York Times* broke the story that in 2007, a Department of Defense program known as the Advanced Aviation Threat Identification Program (AATIP for short; a part of the Advanced Aerospace Weapons System Application Program, or AAWSAP) was established to assess reports of unidentified aerial phenomena (or UAPs, their preferred term for UFOs).

The story also included two videos of UAPs taken by cameras mounted on the

Navy planes, and a third was released a few months later. The videos were recorded in 2004 and 2015 on infrared cameras equipped with target-locking capabilities, and each depicts a small, blurry object seemingly rotating in odd ways or zooming across or accelerating out of the field of view at impossibly fast speeds. The accompanying audio tracks on two of them, with pilots making excited exclamations about what they're seeing, are particularly compelling. Moreover, the story included alleged claims that the United States government was concealing unknown metal alloys that were harvested from crashed UAPs. Needless to say, to the ufology community and ETH believers, this was the moment they had been waiting for, and many were sure the government was about to confirm that UAPs were alien technology.

Almost immediately, however, things started to get messy, and here's where I do my best to break down the major points of a very complicated and convoluted story (perhaps the only kind that exists when it comes to UFOs) from a skeptical perspective. The important points are as follows:

- **Money, money, money:** AAWSAP/AATIP was the pet project of former Nevada senator Harry Reid, who earmarked $22 million for its creation as part of a bill he sponsored. The contract to conduct the investigations was awarded to Bigelow Aerospace, which is owned by Reid's long-time friend, campaign donor, and known UFO and paranormal enthusiast, Robert Bigelow. This was hardly an objective choice to handle such a sensitive subject that has struggled to find scientific acceptance.

- **The "p" actually stands for "paranormal":** In addition to examining the Navy and historical UAP cases, AAWSAP/AATIP also "researched" paranormal and UAP activity at Skinwalker Ranch in Utah, United States (owned by Bigelow at the time), and other fantastical subjects like wormholes, invisibility cloaking, and warp drives. There is some indication that the project was terminated because the Department of Defense was unhappy when they discovered the work their money was actually sponsoring.

• **About those navy videos . . . :** Skeptics were quick to start analyzing the Navy videos that were released with the *Times* story, and it soon became evident they probably weren't as mysterious as they seemed. Especially thorough examinations by independent investigator and science writer Mick West, who used basic geometry and knowledge of how the sensor and tracking technology on the Navy plane's cameras worked, showed that it was very possible they were misidentifications of conventional objects like birds or commercial planes.

There is also a possibility that they were drones or other surveillance crafts belonging to foreign entities, or maybe they were just glitches in the equipment used to record the videos in the first place.

• **Don't blow that whistle:** Luis Elizondo, a former Department of Defense intelligence officer who claimed he was the director for AATIP, was the original whistleblower in 2017. He has gone on to make increasingly sensational claims about the government hiding evidence of extraterrestrials visiting Earth, and in 2022, he was joined by another whistleblower, David Grusch (a former intelligence officer involved in subsequent UAP inquiries).

Grusch testified before Congress in July 2023 about the government recovering alien bodies from UAP crashes and stockpiling alien spacecraft to attempt to reverse engineer their technology. In August 2024, as I'm writing this, news stories are popping up about Elizondo also claiming that the government is hiding alien biological material and that he personally saw an alien implant that was removed from a member of the United States military who had a UAP encounter. In this respect, this UFO renaissance is looking like Roswell all over again.

- **Project Blue Book 2.0+:** Spurred on by the renewed interest, additional government inquiries into UAPs were launched starting in 2020 that included several successive efforts by the Department of Defense, as well as a NASA inquiry that began in 2022, which also established a position for a Director of UAP Research. Several hundred modern UAP sightings have been collected and reviewed, with no hint so far of an extraterrestrial origin.

Oh, and that mystery metal that the government supposedly salvaged from crash sites? A 2024 report released by the Defense Department's ongoing UAP program, the All-Domain Anomaly Resolution Office (AARO), revealed that it was made of regular old Earth metals and probably sourced from an Air Force aircraft.

The somewhat disappointing (but not surprising) result of all of this is that we're more or less back where things left off over fifty years ago in 1969. Once again, a few different government-sponsored organizations have looked into UAP sightings and released reports stating they are likely not related to extraterrestrials, and ufologists still believe there is a cover-up happening. And they might be right that information is being withheld or downplayed in the interest of national security, but again, that doesn't mean aliens, it just means we aren't all entitled to sensitive classified information. An important difference from the past, however, is that some of the stigma about UFOs, or UAPs, or whatever you want to call them has been removed, reporting procedures for UAP sightings are now more standardized, and the book isn't yet closed on these new inquiries.

Out of This World?

Under the basic rules of the scientific method, as with ghost encounters, most UFO "evidence" is not of scientific value because it is based on hearsay, eyewitness accounts, or is just too ambiguous to draw any conclusions from. Government inquiries and scientists agree that most, if not all, UFOs would become IFOs ("I" for "identified") with the right data—or more often, *any* data—on hand. Some additional factors when considering UFO sightings and the ETH from a scientific perspective include:

- **It's a really long trip:** Part of the reason the ETH is so unlikely is that space is just really, really big. Infinitely big. And yes, there are probably an incredibly large number of other planets out there capable of supporting life as we know it, but right now, we don't even know if interstellar travel is possible. If it is, we should consider that even the closest star to us (that isn't our own Sun, obviously), Proxima Centauri, is just over four lightyears away. That's a distance of around twenty-five trillion miles (40 trillion km), which is an awfully long way to travel just to buzz around in our atmosphere for a bit.

  Moreover, an intelligent society that possesses the technology to make that trip in a reasonable amount of time (at least in terms of human lifetimes) would probably also have the technology to observe us undetected or remotely. Why even take the risk of entering our atmosphere?

- **Where to see a UFO:** Richard Medina, a geographer from the University of Utah in Salt Lake City, published a paper in 2023 with a statistical analysis of the most likely places to see UFOs. Medina and his colleagues compiled location data from the

National UFO Reporting Center on sightings from 2001 to 2020 in the continental United States, and then mapped out the hot spots.

They found that UFO sightings were more frequent in areas with less tree cover and less light pollution. These conditions are best met in the western United States, where there are wide open spaces and darker skies. A hot spot was also observed in the far northeastern corner of the country encompassing most of New Hampshire, Vermont, and Maine. Notably, each of these eastern states is associated with a reputation for outdoor recreation, and Maine in particular is host to a Dark Sky Park.

Basically, in places where people are more likely to be spending time outdoors looking at the sky, they're going to see more weird stuff. Another key observation from the study was that the number of sightings also increased near major military installations or airports, suggesting that military and commercial aircraft play a significant role in UFO sightings.

• **Brains are weird:** Errors in our brains' perceptions of what we're seeing, as well as the influence of our beliefs, can make some people see aliens just like others might see ghosts. This is especially relevant when we're talking about the Navy pilots' encounters with UAPs. Ufologists often point to them and commercial pilots as being the gold standard in terms of eyewitnesses, but being a pilot doesn't exempt you from being subject to human error.

Another positive to come out of the recent UAP mania is that there is more openness toward professional pilots coming forward to report any strange things they see. Before, there was a fear that they would be declared unfit to fly if there was a suspicion they were experiencing some sort of hallucination, but we know better now that even perfectly healthy people's eyes and brains can play tricks on them.

- **Natural or man-made phenomena:** Sometimes your gullible brain gets a helping hand because there are *so many* natural and man-made phenomena that can be mistaken as UFOs. These include but are not limited to: planets (often Venus, which can appear particularly bright), satellites, rocket launches, lenticular clouds, weather balloons, meteors, comets, mirages, birds, planes, and drones.

ALIEN ABDUCTIONS

Alien abductions are often seen as an extension of UFO phenomena but deserve separate consideration, because while it is one thing to see something weird in the sky, it is quite another to believe you've been kidnapped by extraterrestrials. After flying saucer sightings took off in the late 1940s, there were a few questionable reports of individuals who were contacted by aliens (usually with the theme of discouraging us from using nuclear weapons), and even abduction claims, but once again, the phenomenon truly started because of a single influential story.

Alien Abduction Insurance

In 1987, Mike St. Lawrence of Altamonte Springs, Florida, United States, and owner of Saint Lawrence Agency, became the first and exclusive offerer of a novelty alien abduction insurance policy. The insurance payout was $10 million, paid in installments of $1 a year over ten million years for policyholders with a "valid" claim. Mark offered the policy for an economical one-time payment of $24.95 — what a steal! Filing a claim required one simple thing; the claimant needed to obtain a signature from the onboard aliens at the time of abduction.

In a 2019 interview with Leader's Edge, Mike St. Lawrence said he had a total of seven thousand policy holders and two accepted claims. One of those claims was accepted only after the alleged abductee submitted a dark photograph. Written in the margins of the photo was, "Sorry, but the lighting was really dark inside the UFO." When asked about it in the interview, Mike said, "To me that was genius on his part . . . He deserves $1 a year for sure."

Unfortunately, it seems the Saint Lawrence Agency is no longer operational (or at the very least the webpage no longer works). As far as I can tell there are no legitimate alien abduction policies available for purchase, but if they don't exist yet I suspect it is only a matter of time before they do.

BETTY AND BARNEY'S WILD RIDE

◆◆◆

Newlyweds Betty and Barney Hill were returning from a belated honeymoon trip to Montreal, Canada, on the night of September 19, 1961, when something incredibly strange happened. Around 10:30 p.m., while driving through the White Mountains just south of Lancaster, New Hampshire, United States, Betty noticed a bright light in the sky. They stopped the car for Betty to take a look using their binoculars, through which she thought the object looked like a "spinning disk." Barney, on the other hand, initially believed it was just a plane.

The Hills kept driving but stopped again a short time later, as it seemed like they were now being pursued by this mysterious, glowing craft, which by that point appeared to be hovering nearby. Barney grabbed his gun and the binoculars and jumped out of the car to take another look. He walked toward the object, which he could see now was a huge, pancake-shaped craft with a row of windows (so, a flying saucer), and when he stopped about fifty feet (15 m) away to take another look with the binoculars, he observed many strange figures in black uniforms staring back at him. Barney tried to raise his gun (shoot first, ask questions later—the American way!) but found himself unable to do so, which seems like a pretty normal freeze response to fear. In a state of panic, Barney fled back to the car, and the Hills took off down the road, leaving the craft behind, or so they thought.

A short time later, Betty and Barney reported feeling drowsy, and then all of a sudden they woke up thirty-five miles (56 km) further down the road, two hours later, with no recollection of what had happened during that time. Betty's dress was torn and stained, Barney's shoes were scuffed, the binocular's strap was broken, and both of their watches had stopped working. They also claimed their car had odd, polished spots on the trunk that would make a compass needle spin, but the spots faded away within a few months. (Note that I cannot find any official confirmation of the stopped watches or magnetized car trunk, and with respect to the car, it should be considered that iron-rich metal, such as the steel in cars, can affect the behavior of compasses and is not evidence of radiation, as Betty thought.)

Scared and confused, Betty put in a call to a friend who worked at Pease Air Force Base, Major Paul Henderson, and reported the ordeal as a UFO sighting. Amazingly, Henderson found that two nearby Air Force installations also recorded radar sightings of UFOs from that same night, and all three were logged as part of Project Blue Book (although the additional sightings were later debunked as being inconsistent with the timeline described by the Hills). Betty also reported the sighting to the now defunct National Investigations Committee on Aerial Phenomena (NICAP).

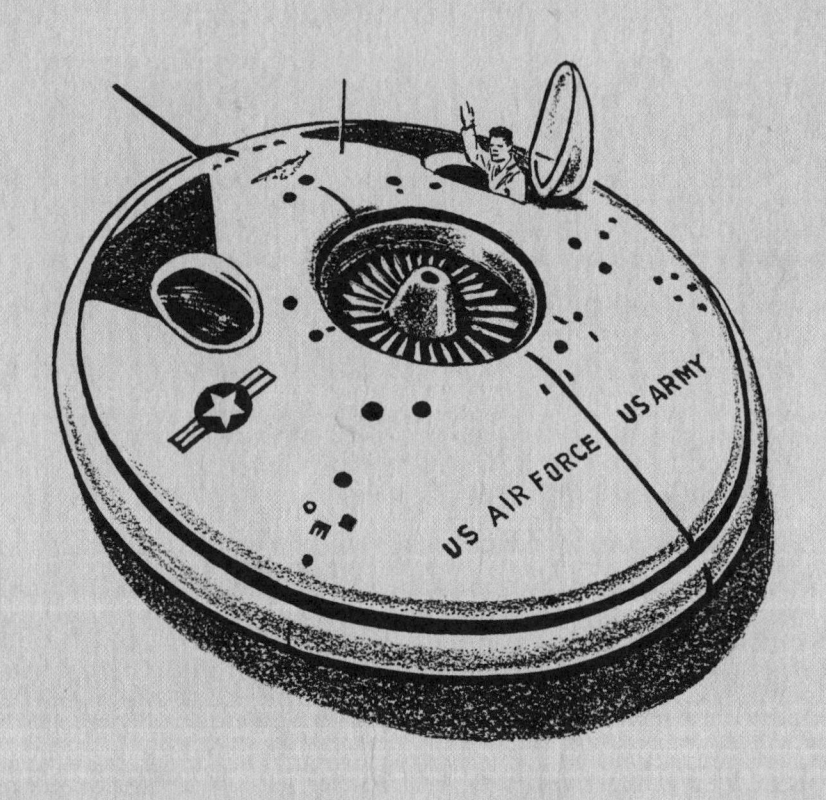

Nightmares and Hypnosis, or How to Create an Alien Abduction

◆◆◆

Betty, convinced she and Barney witnessed a UFO, immediately began researching other encounters at the local library. Within a couple of weeks, she started having vivid nightmares about a harrowing abduction that neither she nor Barney consciously remembered from that fateful mid-September night. She wrote everything down, including details like having a long needle inserted into her belly button, the aliens examining both her and Barney's genitals, and a star map the aliens showed her. From these dreams, Betty also laid out a general order of events that occurred, starting with the aliens blocking the couple in the road and escorting them into the ship and then into separate exam rooms to commence a large number of medical tests.

In 1963, Barney, who also suffered from sleep problems and anxiety, decided to see a psychiatrist. Together, he and Betty were referred to Dr. Benjamin Simon, who specialized in hypnosis, to see if he might help the Hills remember what happened during the missing time from the night of their UFO sighting. In separate sessions, Betty and Barney recalled very similar stories of being taken into an alien spacecraft and experimented on, with many details that matched those Betty dreamed and wrote about earlier. The aliens they described were the stereotypical gray beings with large eyes and bald heads that most people are familiar with today.

From a skeptical angle, it's important to note that most versions of the Hills' story fail to mention the details of Betty's dreams and imply that none of their memories of the supposed abduction were accessed until these later hypnosis sessions. This makes it seem much more remarkable that their stories were such a good match, when in reality it's likely because Betty was writing and talking at length with Barney about her dreams in the intervening two years between the abduction and their initial psychiatrist visit. And even without the influence of Betty's dreams, we know now that memory recovery under hypnosis (or hypnotic regression therapy) is at best controversial, and at worst, can actually plant false, traumatic memories in people's brains.

Furthermore, Betty had a sister who had previously reported a UFO encounter, and we know she spent a lot of time reading and thinking about the phenomenon and likely sharing her thoughts with Barney. Any way you look at it, the psychological ingredients were there for the Hills to create an alien abduction story, and Dr. Simon, their psychiatrist, agreed.

THE STANDARD IS SET

Betty and Barney Hill's abduction story essentially set the standard for all future abduction narratives. As you probably noticed, it contains many of the classic abduction story tropes, such as mysterious bright lights, hovering aircraft, missing time (which I know we haven't addressed yet, but we will on page 185), medical experimentation, gray aliens (often just called "Grays"), and the recovery of repressed memories. The Hills' abduction experience was chronicled in a 1966 book by John G. Fuller called *The Interrupted Journey*, as well as a popular 1975 TV movie starring James Earl Jones and Estelle Parsons called *The UFO Incident*. This movie may have played a role in at least one other famous alien abduction story, as it's been suggested that it gave Travis Walton the idea to fake his own abduction to help his future brother-in-law avoid trouble with a logging contract they were running late on. Honestly, you have to at least give him points for creativity.

For the most part, the subsequent experiences recounted by abductees continued to follow a very similar format to that laid out by Betty and Barney Hill, with problematic variability in the details, as mentioned earlier. In the late 1960s, alien implants were introduced into the narrative with the abduction of Betty Andreasson, though they always seem to magically disappear after they are removed from abductees or turn out to be something mundane. Susan Blackmore, a professor and parapsychologist interested in alien abductions, had another suspected implant analyzed using x-ray spectroscopy, and it ended up being nothing more than a dental filling that had fallen out.

Moving forward, the 1980s and 1990s saw renewed interest in abductions with the release of several popular books written by both abductees and ufologists. Of particular note are books by ufologists Budd Hopkins, David Jacobs, and John Mack, who all claimed they helped abductees reclaim lost memories via hypnotic regression. Only one of the three, Mack, was a trained psychiatrist, and he was widely criticized by his colleagues for reinforcing, and potentially adding to, his patients' beliefs that they were abducted. As for Hopkins and Jacobs, there are obviously serious ethical concerns with untrained individuals utilizing a psychiatric technique that has the potential to plant false, traumatic memories into people's minds. Also, as a rule, I try not to let myself be hypnotized by people who think aliens are abducting people to create a race of alien-human hybrids (a belief held by both Hopkins and Jacobs).

The Science Behind "Alien Abductions"

I've stated that the Hills' supposed abduction experience was the inspiration for most others past that point, but I want to clarify that this doesn't mean I think other abductees are necessarily lying, nor do I think Betty and Barney were lying. Sure, there are hoaxes out there, but there are also psychological and environmental factors that can trick someone into believing they were abducted by aliens. What follows is a summary of some of these possibilities.

False Memory Syndrome

The exact numbers vary, but overall, psychological research suggests that false memories, meaning memories of events that didn't actually happen, are fairly common, or at least that a significant percentage of people are quite susceptible to having them implanted via methods like hypnosis. In 2002, a team of Harvard researchers led by Susan A. Clancy evaluated the susceptibility of self-proclaimed alien abductees to false memory creation. In the simple but effective experiment, participants were read a series of words and then asked to recall as many of them as they could a short time later after completing a few simple math problems. The words were all related in some way and associated with what the researchers called a "critical lure" word. For example, for a list containing words like "sour, candy, sugar, bitter, good, taste, tooth, nice, honey," and so forth, the critical lure is "sweet."

Participants with recovered memories of alien abductions were more likely to include the lure word when asked to recall what words they remembered hearing. This suggests that abductees are more likely to invent false memories. However, that doesn't mean they are any less terrifying or less real for those affected. Other studies have shown that abductees respond in physiologically and emotionally similar ways as post-traumatic stress disorder (PTSD) patients when their experiences are recounted back to them.

Memories of Accidental Awareness

Accidental awareness occurs when a patient wakes up from general anesthesia and is able to see and/or hear what is happening during surgery—an experience that I imagine is more horrifying than almost anything we've talked about in this book. Psychoanalyst David V. Forrest proposed that stories from abductees about waking up on tables with bright lights and strange figures crowded around them performing medical procedures could very well be mixed up memories about an accidental awareness event. A report on hundreds of accidental awareness events compiled by the Royal College of Anesthetists in London (United Kingdom) indicates that affected patients experienced pain, feelings of helplessness, and panic, and over 40 percent were left with lasting psychological effects, including PTSD. Some of their accounts make even alien abductions seem restful in comparison.

SLEEP PARALYSIS

One of the more common variations of the abduction narrative introduced by the Hills is that the abductee wakes up in their bed unable to move and feeling panicked. They might see strange lights, hear odd noises, or even see or sense some type of being(s) in the room with them. This probably sounds very familiar to how a large number of ghost encounters start (see page 47), and once again, we can thank sleep paralysis. Turns out some sleep paralysis demons are ghosts, some are bogeymen, and others are aliens.

Although sleep paralysis has been formally recognized by the American Academy of Sleep Medicine since 1979, that didn't stop Budd Hopkins, David Jacobs, and Ron Westrum (a sociologist and Mutual UFO Network, or MUFON, consultant) from including "waking up paralyzed with a sense of a strange person or presence or something else in the room" as an indicator of an alien abduction in a 1991 Roper poll.

ENVIRONMENTAL FACTORS AND MISSING TIME/AMNESIA

As with ghosts, environmental factors that increase the risk of hallucinatory experiences may be a factor in alien abduction claims. In particular, carbon monoxide exposure can cause memory loss in some individuals and can be present both in homes and in cars. A dangerous buildup of the deadly gas can occur in cars for several reasons, including emission system or engine problems, holes in the body of the vehicle, or driving with the trunk open.

The trunk detail makes me wonder if carbon monoxide played a role in Betty and Barney Hill's missing time. The original NICAP report says Barney retrieved the gun from the trunk on their final stop, so maybe in the rush to drive away, they left the trunk of their car open. Carbon monoxide began accumulating in the cab of the car, making them both feel irresistibly tired, and Benny had the wherewithal to pull off on the side of the road at some point but didn't remember it.

Alternatively, in the excitement of stopping to look at the UFO, they simply lost track of time and then were surprised by how late it was once things settled down. Either way, given that the missing time wasn't actually noticed until a few weeks after the incident when they were questioned by ufologists, and Betty was already quite upset by that point, it might have seemed much more nefarious than it actually was.

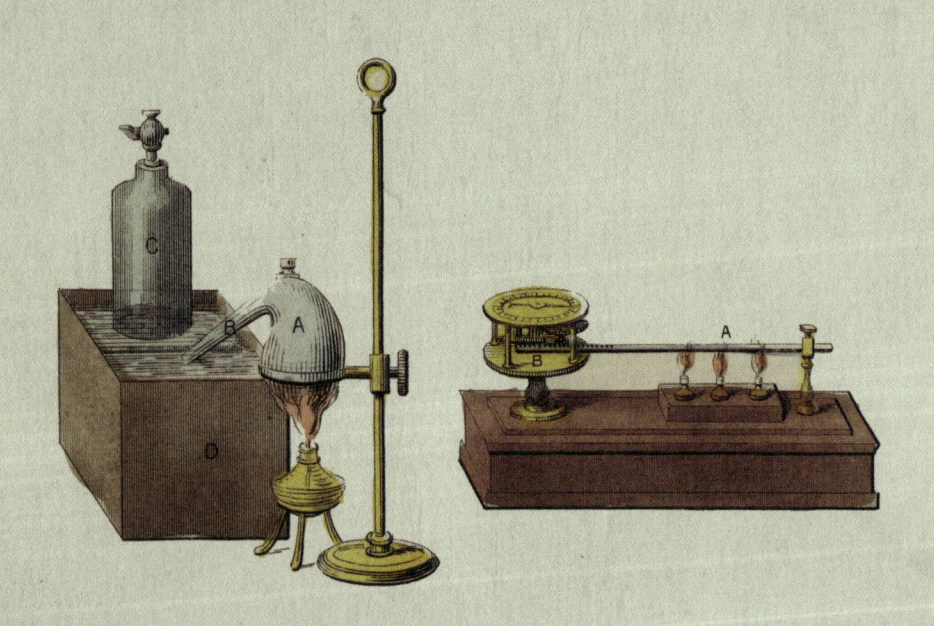

CROP CIRCLES

Crop circles, a term coined in the early 1980s, are large-scale patterns that are flattened into fields of wheat, corn, or other grains. As the name implies, they are often based around a geometric design featuring whole or partial circular shapes. They typically mysteriously appear overnight and are intended to be visible from the sky, and it's for these reasons that cereologists (people who study crop circles) and by extension, ufologists, believe that they are another sign of extraterrestrial visitation. In the early 1990s, they were revealed to be hoaxes, and today, people mainly see them as works of art. However, if comment sections on social media have taught me anything, it's that a lot of people still have very strong opinions about the otherworldly origin of crop circles than I ever would have imagined.

Early "Crop Circles": Devils, Vortices, and Nests

Early "crop circles" were wholly different from the enormous, geometrically complex works of art that are produced today. According to cereologists, the first recorded one is depicted in a pamphlet published in 1678 titled *The Mowing-Devil: or, Strange News Out of Hartford-Shire*. The image in the pamphlet shows a devil figure cutting a field of oats using a scythe in an oval-shaped pattern, working from the outer edges of the field inward. The accompanying story is about a farmer who refused to pay a laborer to harvest his field of oats, declaring that he would rather have the devil himself cut the field than pay the laborer a fair price for the job. Next thing the farmer knew, Satan showed up in the middle of the night to call his bluff, leaving him too terrified to actually collect and sell the harvested crop.

While it seems pretty clear that this was a fable meant to warn against miserliness, cereologists argue that *The Mowing Devil* is based on an actual event that seventeenth-century people attributed to the work of the devil, as they couldn't conceive of aliens at the time. But even if we entertain the thought that this actually happened, the crop circle story doesn't hold up. It would seem more likely that the "devil" who cut the field was really someone trying to scare the farmer for refusing to pay a fair price. Additionally, the crops were *cut*, not laid down in a circular pattern as is characteristic of true crop circles.

Other early "crop circles" appear to be of natural origins. One example comes from a letter published in 1880 in the now prominent scientific journal *Nature*. In it, author John Capron describes circular spots observed in wheat fields and attributes them to "cyclonic wind action." Then, in 1963, an astronomer named Patrick Moore was examining what he believed to be a meteor impact crater in a field in Wiltshire, England, when he noticed circular or oval-shaped areas of flattened wheat laid down in a spiral pattern. He wasn't sure what caused them and didn't find any meteorite pieces, but he thought the flattened areas could be related to strong air currents produced by whatever created the impact crater. Notably, we don't have any photographs or concrete evidence beyond eyewitness testimony about these circles.

The final example is the "flying saucer nest" that showed up in reeds (not crops) growing in a marshy lagoon on an Australian farm in 1966, accompanied by a UFO sighting. In this case, however, the reeds weren't bent over, but were uprooted and swirled around into a floating mat, leading meteorologists to debunk them as the result of a weather event like a waterspout (known to occur in the area) or strong down-draft. Although these had a more obvious natural explanation than the 1880 and 1963 "crop circles," the story spread internationally, and "flying saucer nests" began showing up in England.

Randy Hedgehogs

One of the early theories about crop circles (aka "corn circles") in the 1980s was that small animals were creating patterns in the crops while running in or feeding on them. Hedgehogs were considered possible culprits of the circles as a result of their strange mating dance. When a male hedgehog (boar) finds a female hedgehog (sow) they deem worthy of pursuing, the boar will begin chasing the sow in circles repeatedly; this occurs after his initial advances are rejected. This chase continues until the sow is thoroughly impressed by the boar's stamina—this can take several hours. The hedgehogs repetitively run over the same spots, leaving flattened grass behind, typically in a circular pattern.

The hedgehog theory is one of our favorites; however, creating patterns in large fields of crops would take pretty sizable hedgehogs, and the intricate nature of many of the designs would also require them to be extremely intelligent. Fortunately for us (or maybe unfortunately?), we do not have giant, highly intelligent hedgehogs walking among us. The hedgehog's limited size and inability to create intricate art are just a couple of reasons why the randy hedgehog theory didn't stick.

Doug and Dave's Alien Adventure

If this section has a theme outside of aliens, it's that all it takes is one person (or in this case, two people) to change the course of human history. When it comes to the crop circle phenomena, those people were a pair of friends named Doug Bower and Dave Chorley, who, in 1991, confessed that they had started the modern crop circle craze in 1978 and had since created over two hundred of them across the English countryside around the counties of Hampshire and Wiltshire. Bower and Chorley came up with the idea while having a drink (or maybe a few) in a pub one night in 1978. They heard about Australia's "flying saucer nests" and decided it would be hilarious to create one in an attempt to fool everyone into thinking a UFO had landed in the English countryside.

And fool everyone they did, for the next twelve years. Bower and Chorley explained to the media that all it took to make their increasingly intricate designs were wooden boards attached to pieces of rope that they could step on to flatten down the plants without breaking the stalks. The perfect circles were simply made by anchoring a piece of string at the center and traversing around it while keeping the string taut. They even did a demonstration and created a design for the London tabloid *Today*, who then called in a crop circle expert to examine it. The expert assessed the design and declared no human could have created it, and then the tabloid reporter introduced him to Bower and Chorley. Big. Oof.

Bower and Chorley's decision to confess came after they realized cereologists were going after government funding to support their research, causing their guilt to finally win out. By then, their practical joke was the inspiration for an entire movement of copycat pranksters and artists (who now call themselves circlemakers) that spread around the world, with circles that showed up across Europe, Russia, North America, Japan, Indonesia, and

India. Hundreds of other crop circles were made in addition to the two hundred from Bower and Chorley leading up to their 1991 confession. To date, over ten thousand crop circles have appeared worldwide.

Modern Crop Circles

Crop circles continue to appear today and have gotten more complex as circlemakers challenge themselves to make larger, more elaborate designs within the constraints of a single night (although some do take multiple nights to create). This has been made easier with the advent of GPS technology, drones, and laser grids that can help groups map things out and coordinate as they work on a new circle. Some of the most famous circles include a six-hundred-foot-wide (183 m) representation of a fractal pattern known as the Julia set, a geometric representation of the first ten digits of pi, which required decoding by an astrophysicist, and even a supposed response to the Arecibo message that was beamed into space using the Arecibo Radio Telescope in 1974. The largest design made to date appeared in Wiltshire, England, in 2001 and was nine hundred feet (274 m) across. As of 2021, it was reported that an average of thirty circles appear per year in the United Kingdom, which continues to be their most popular location..

The Science of Crop Circles

At the end of the day, crop circles are likely created by human beings, but there have been various "scientific" attempts to link them to strange natural phenomena or to advanced or alien technology over the years. Several natural phenomena have been proposed to explain modern crop circles, including a resurrection of the wind vortices hypothesis from 1880 (later amended to an "electro-magneto-hydrodynamic 'plasma vortex,'" whatever that means), ball lightning, or even that Earth's magnetic field somehow energizes the crops into collapsing into distinct patterns. In general though, as crop circles became more and more complex, natural explanations (which arguably were more supernatural) were largely abandoned by cereologists.

From 1994 to 2001, a few biophysicists (W.C. Levengood, N.P. Talbott, and E.H. Haselhoff) published academic papers in which they claimed they found evidence that electromagnetic radiation was used to heat the wheat stalks in crop circles, causing the viscoelastic joints along them to elongate and bend the plant over. Rebuttals point out that natural causes can create swelling in stalk joints and that elongation is also expected during manual flattening of stalks (like with boards), but one interesting possibility suggested by physicist Richard Taylor is that it represents a change in circlemakers' techniques. He proposes that circlemakers may be using handheld microwave generators or creating homemade versions by removing the magnetrons from microwave ovens to quickly heat and bend the wheat stalks, allowing them to make more and more complex designs at a faster pace.

Overall, while some cereologists and ufologists continue to push the idea that a subset of crop circles are impossible to create by humans, the fact is that human circlemakers demonstrate again and again that they are capable of making these intricate works of art. The belief that aliens have the advanced technology to travel across trillions and trillions of miles of space only to leave us cryptic messages in our corn and wheat fields when they get here is, in all honesty, pretty silly. Surely a civilization with technology that far ahead of our own would conceive of a less ambiguous way to communicate? Or maybe at this point they're up there having a laugh just like Doug and Dave.

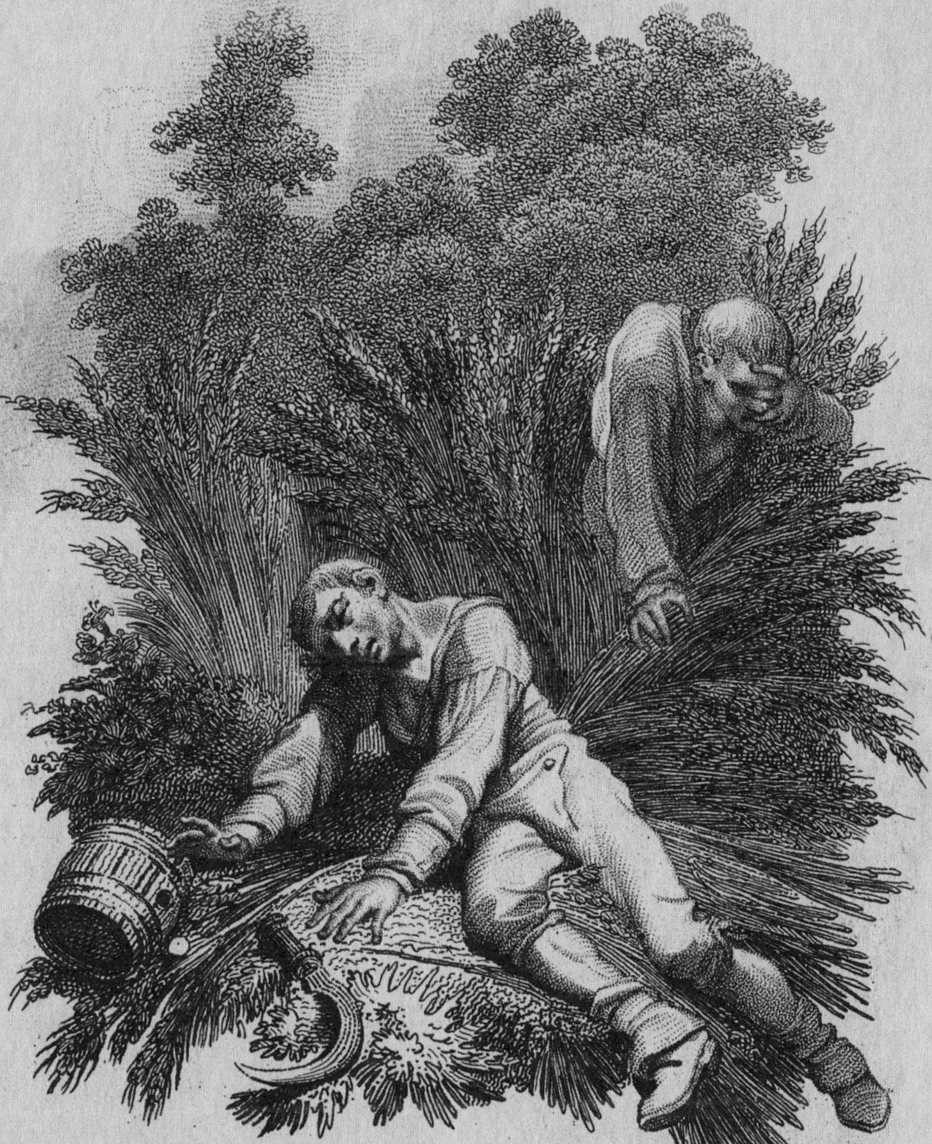

Something Spooky

When I was a teenager, I was almost abducted by aliens, or at least that's what I thought late one night when I was sleeping on my aunt and uncle's couch in rural Ohio. I was trying to fall asleep when I heard something fly over the house and then continue out across the corn field behind it. When the mystery craft reached the other side of the field, it turned and shone an incredibly bright light into the house. As you can imagine, my thirteen-year-old brain, with many seasons of *The X-Files* under its belt, was convinced that I was about to be levitated out across the corn field into the alien mothership.

What I saw was likely a search helicopter. I must have been half asleep when it passed over the house the first time, so I didn't identify the sound. The helicopter was probably equipped with an infrared camera, detected the heat signature of a neighbor's dog on the porch, and then shined a spotlight to check that it wasn't whoever they were looking for. And in retrospect, I probably should have been more afraid of the possibility that there was someone dangerous on the loose in the area.

Test Your Knowledge

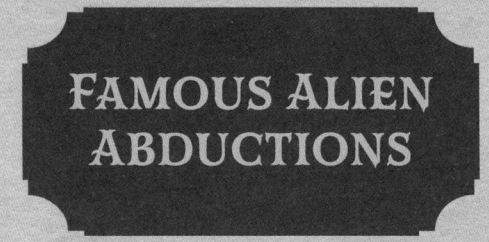

Famous Alien Abductions

Below are some brief descriptions of famous alien abduction stories. Can you guess which famous stories these descriptions are referring to? What are the similarities between these stories and the story of Betty and Barney Hill?

A. A logger from Snowflake, Arizona, United States, was allegedly abducted during the winter of 1975, when he and his six friends were driving home from a project in the Apache-Sitgreaves National Forest. The story was the inspiration for the film *Fire in the Sky* as well as a feature in several alien and UFO documentaries. It is considered one of the most famous alien abduction stories to date.

B. Detailed in the 1996 book *Encounter*, an alien abduction occurred when a couple was driving home around midnight. They saw (for the second time) a flying disc with bright lights. It then landed on the side of the road and they, as well as another car of people in the area, approached it — as one does when one sees a mysterious flying disc. The abductee claims their memory blanked and they woke up several hundred meters down the road, but through hypnosis they were reminded of what happened next.

Answers on page 203

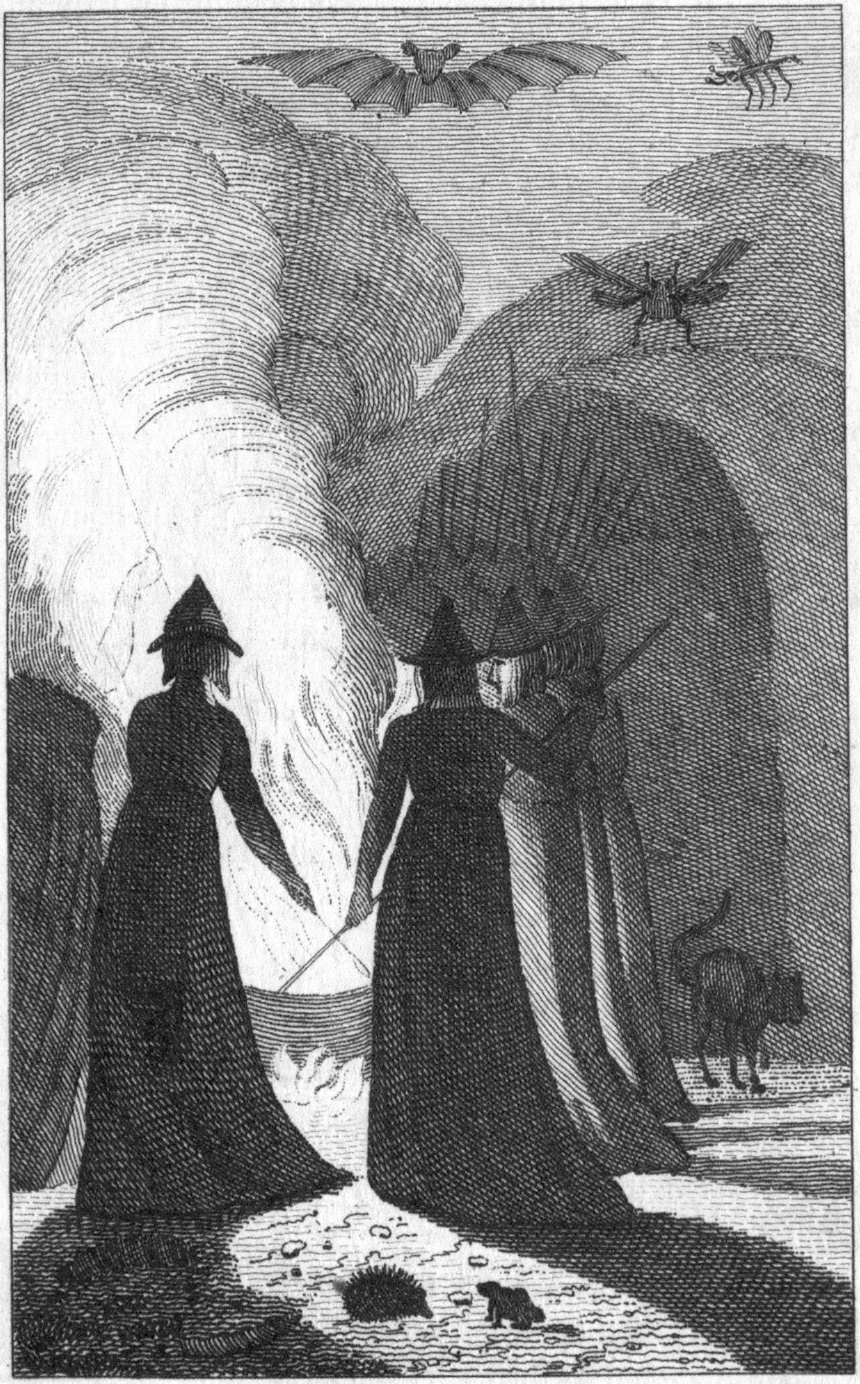

CONCLUSION

We have arrived at the end of our science-based exploration of some of the most popular paranormal phenomena. When Paige and I started *Spooky Science Sisters*, my supernatural podcast consumption was pretty much limited to those that suspend disbelief and skepticism to tell a good scary story, and I was determined to do something different. The goal was to create a space for people like me, who love those stories, but have trouble accepting them at face value.

I was convinced that we would find stories that resisted all attempts at debunking, or at least a few examples of valid scientific evidence for the existence of some paranormal thing, but so far, they don't exist. The more I learn about all the possible scientific or logical explanations that could be behind people's supernatural experiences, the more skeptical I become. And after getting to do even deeper dives into the origins and explanations for paranormal phenomena for this book, any lingering doubts I might have had vanished faster than Bloody Mary when the bathroom light is switched on.

Finding irrefutable evidence for a paranormal phenomenon like ghosts or intelligent extraterrestrial life visiting Earth would be one of the biggest scientific discoveries of all time. It would fundamentally change what we know about our world and our place in it, which means the standard of proof must also be high. Of course, that means doing things by the book using the scientific method. Importantly, this doesn't mean we have to box ourselves in (a common criticism from believers). While my current hypothesis is that there is nothing paranormal going on in this world, I would be happy to be proven wrong someday. In the meantime, though, keep an eye on those weird brains of yours, and as always, stay spooky.

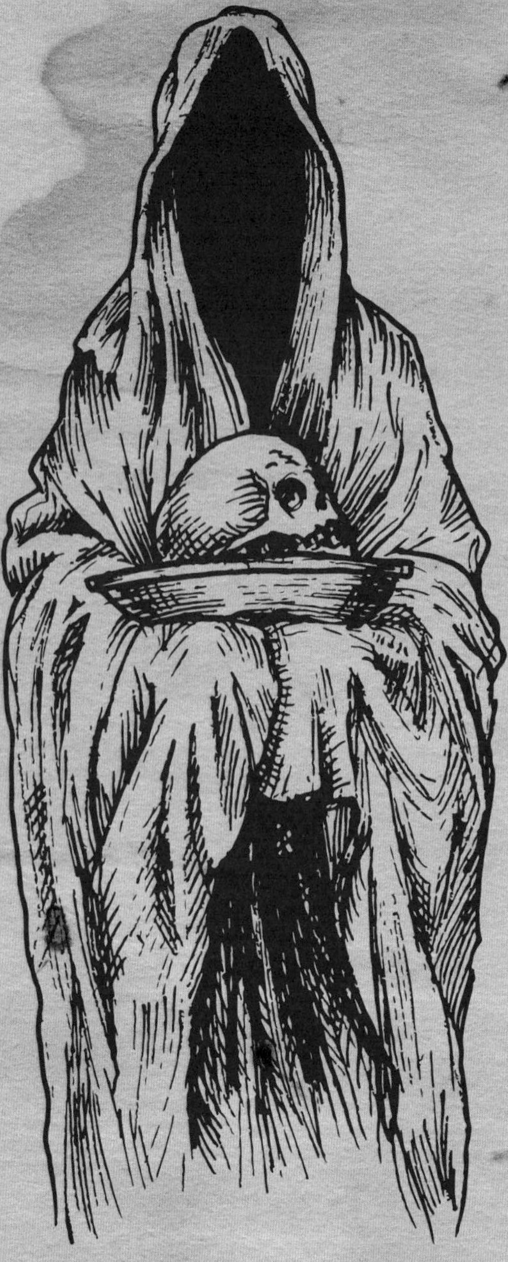

Test Your Knowledge Answer Key

HAUNTED HOUSES (PAGE 55)

A. The Winchester Mystery House (also known as the Winchester Mansion) in San Jose, California, United States. Sarah Winchester, owner of the house and inheritor of her late husband's fortune (from the Winchester Arms Company), was interested in architecture and used a small portion of her fortune on building the mansion. The stories of endless construction and "vengeful spirits" began at a rumored meeting with a medium—for which there is no record. And the "endless construction" was not so endless after all; there are records indicating that they started and stopped several times during construction. The strange house features were likely a result of the 1906 earthquake in San Francisco that caused portions of the house to collapse. Instead of rebuilding those sections of home, Sarah chose to seal them off, resulting in stairs and doors leading nowhere.

B. The Stanley Hotel in Estes Park, Colorado. Several unfortunate events have occurred over the years at the Stanley Hotel, including when an employee lit a candle during a gas leak, causing an explosion (reports say it occurred near room 217—one of the rooms they now consider "spirited"). The power of suggestion (see page 37) likely plays a part in the more recent haunting stories of the Stanley Hotel. The history of the hotel, deaths that occurred inside the rooms, and Stephen King's experience (and book) have given the hotel a reputation that influences how experiences are perceived by new visitors.

MONSTER MADNESS (PAGE 103)

A. Frankenstein's Monster. The 1818 novel *Frankenstein; or, the Modern Prometheus* was written by a young Mary Shelley in response to her friend and poet Lord Byron's challenge to a group of friends to write the most haunting scary story. The story has proven to be one of the most influential works of horror and fiction and has over thirty film, television, and play adaptations. In addition to its influence in literature and film, the story has served as a framework to the scientific community about ethical responsibility in medical and other scientific research.

B. Zombies. Most of us would agree that zombies, at least in the undead "braaaiins" sense, do not exist. But society still fears the possibility of a future zombie outbreak—so much so that several books and guides exist offering advice on what to do if one occurs. From a medical standpoint, the traditional Hollywood zombie apocalypse is not really plausible, but an outbreak of a highly transmissible disease with "zombielike" symptoms may not be totally out of the realm of possibility. According to Dr. Steven Scholzman, Harvard Medical School professor and psychiatrist, a man-made pathogen that increases hunger and reduces higher brain function is the most likely zombie outbreak scenario.

CREEPING CRYPTIDS (PAGE 137)

A. Animal. The kangaroo! Kangaroos were believed to be cryptids until the late eighteenth century when Sir Joseph Banks brought a skin of the kangaroo back to England after his participation on Captain Cook's Endeavor voyage.

B. Animal. The thylacine (aka the Tasmanian Tiger or Tasmanian Wolf)! Before the last known thylacine died in 1936, it could be found in Tasmania.

Thylacines were officially designated "extinct" in 1986. However, hundreds of unconfirmed sightings have been reported since then, some of which were as recent as 2023. While it is believed that the thylacine is extinct now, there is research suggesting that the true extinction date of these marsupials may have been a bit later than 1986.

Eerie Urban Legends (page 159)

A. Dyatlov Pass. For decades there have been questions about what happened to the hikers of Dyatlov Pass. Theories ranging from aliens and yetis to Soviet government conspiracies all surrounded this story. In 2019 the investigation was reopened, and it was determined that a change in weather likely caused an avalanche, leading to the death of the hikers — either by fractures from the dense snow slabs or by the extreme temperatures causing frostbite and hypothermia.

B. The Hat Man. A sleep paralysis demon that made its rounds in the creepypasta-verse for almost two decades before the 2020 resurgence and Benadryl Challenge. Taking Benadryl will help you sleep (or should I say, *make* you sleep), but at large enough doses it can cause hallucinations, confusion, and other symptoms that can increase your chances of experiencing sleep paralysis and, therefore improve your chances of seeing the Hat Man. Overdosing on Benadryl can even cause death — and it did for one teenager during the 2020 Hat Man trend. Importantly, the Hat Man is not a supernatural entity, and he is not real. The Hat Man is just a run-of-the-mill sleep paralysis hallucination. Write stories about him if you'd like, but please do not take large doses of Benadryl (or encourage others to do so) in an attempt to summon him.

FAMOUS ALIEN ABDUCTIONS (PAGE 195)

A. The abduction story of Travis Walton. The group reports seeing a bright light and flying saucer in the sky while driving during the night (sound familiar?). They claim that when Walton approached the saucer, a beam of light shone down, he lost consciousness, and the saucer disappeared.

However, there is no physical evidence of the alleged abduction and as famous as the story is, most skeptics, as well as some believers, think it was nothing more than a hoax. Walton had several motives for faking an abduction, which included avoiding large penalties for not promptly completing his team's logging work and *The National Enquirer*'s offering of $5,000 for the winning UFO story of the year—it should come as no surprise that Walton's story was published and received the prize money.

B. The abduction story of Kelly Cahill. Bill Chalker, a UFO investigator from Sydney, Australia, worked on Cahill's abduction investigation and put her in contact with a group called Phenomena Research Australia (PRA). When they interviewed the people from the second car, their stories matched Cahill's, and they reported having the same strange marks on their bodies that Cahill had on hers. The report, detailing all of this, which was supposedly three hundred pages in the late 1990s, is still being withheld by the PRA.

In 1998, Cahill published her book and was involved in a series of TV appearances, talks, and conferences. Yet no matter how much publicity Cahill and her story got, her husband and the other witnesses refused to come out publicly with their stories—a red flag in the eyes of skeptics. Eventually, in 1998 Kelly Cahill disappeared and so did interest in her story. Some believers think Cahill's story was a lost opportunity or the alien abduction "holy grail." Though with no official report, no physical evidence, and no public witness statements, it's hard to believe this was anything more than a well-planned hoax.

SELECTED BIBLIOGRAPHY

PART I: THINGS THAT GO "BOO!" IN THE NIGHT

Dagnall, Neil, Kenneth G. Drinkwater, Ciarán O'Keeffe, Annalisa Ventola, Brian Laythe, Michael A. Jawer, Brandon Massullo, Giovanni B. Caputo, and James Houran. "Things That Go Bump in the Literature: An Environmental Appraisal of 'Haunted Houses.'" *Frontiers in Psychology* 11 (June 12, 2020): 1328. doi.org/10.3389/fpsyg.2020.01328.

Felton, D. *Haunted Greece and Rome: Ghost Stories from Classical Antiquity*. Austin, TX: University of Texas Press, 1999. doi.org/10.7560/725072.

Finkel, Irving L. *The First Ghosts*. London: Hodder & Stoughton, 2019.

French, Chris. *The Science of Weird Shit: Why Our Minds Conjure the Paranormal*. Cambridge, Massachusetts: The MIT Press, 2024.

Lange, Rense, and James Houran. "Context-Induced Paranormal Experiences: Support for Houran and Lange's Model of Haunting Phenomena." *Perceptual and Motor Skills* 84, no. 3 (June 1997): 1455–58. doi.org/10.2466 pms.1997.84.3c.1455.

Morton, Lisa. *Ghosts: A Haunted History*. London: Reaktion Books, 2015.

Peoples, Hervey C., Pavel Duda, and Frank W. Marlowe. "Hunter-Gatherers and the Origins of Religion." *Human Nature (Hawthorne, N.Y.)* 27 (2016): 261–82. doi.org/10.1007/s12110-016-9260-0.

Radford, Benjamin. *Investigating Ghosts: The Scientific Search for Spirits*. First edition. Coralles, New Mexico: Rhombus Publishing Company, 2017.

Roach, Mary. *Six Feet Over: Science Tackles the Afterlife*. New York: W.W. Norton & Company, 2022.

Wiseman, R., C. Watt, E. Greening, P. Stevens, and C. O'Kefffe. "An Investigation into the Alleged Haunting of Hampton Court Palace: Psychological Variables and Magnetic Fields," 2002. uhra.herts.ac.uk/handle/2299/2280.

Wiseman, Richard. *Paranormality: Why We See What Isn't There*. London: Spin Solutions Ltd., 2010.

PART II: CREEPY CREATURES AND LEGENDARY FEATURES

Bader, Christopher. "The UFO Contact Movement from the 1950's to the Present." *Sociology Faculty Articles and Research* 17, no. 2 (January 1, 1995): 73–90.

Barber, Paul. *Vampires, Burial, and Death: Folklore and Reality*. New Haven, CT: Yale University Press, 2010. www.jstor.org/stable/j.ctt1nq6gm.

Beresford, Matthew. *The White Devil: The Werewolf in European Culture*. Chicago: Reaktion Books, 2013.

Blackmore, Susan. "Abduction by Aliens or Sleep Paralysis?" *Skeptical Inquirer*, June 1998.

Blécourt, Willem de. "Monstrous Theories: Werewolves and the Abuse of History." *Preternature: Critical and Historical Studies on the Preternatural* 2, no. 2 (2013): 188–212. doi.org/10.5325/preternature.2.2.0188.

Caputo, Giovanni B. "Strange-Face-in-the-Mirror Illusion." *Perception* 39, no. 7 (July 1, 2010): 1007–8. doi.org/10.1068/p6466.

Clancy, Susan A., Richard J. McNally, Daniel L. Schacter, Mark F. Lenzenweger, and Roger K. Pitman. "Memory Distortion in People Reporting Abduction by Aliens." *Journal of Abnormal Psychology* 111, no. 3 (2002): 455–61. doi.org/10.1037/0021-843X.111.3.455.

Dunning, Brian. "The Black Eyed Kids." *Skeptoid*, April 15, 2014. skeptoid.com/episodes/4410.

Eghigian, Greg. *After the Flying Saucers Came: A Global History of the UFO Phenomenon*. New York: Oxford University Press, 2024.

Foxon, Floe. "Bigfoot: If It's There, Could It Be a Bear?" *Journal of Zoology* 323, no. 1 (2024): 1–8. doi.org/10.1111/jzo.13148.

Foxon, Floe. "The Loch Ness Monster: If It's Real, Could It Be an Eel?" *JMIRx Bio* 1, no. 1 (July 21, 2023): e49063. doi.org/10.2196/49063.

Frank, Adam. *The Little Book of Aliens*. New York: HarperCollins Publishers, 2023.

Hallab, Mary. "Vampires and Medical Science." *The Journal of Popular Culture* 48, no. 1 (February 2015): 168–83. doi.org/10.1111/jpcu.12241.

Kusche, Larry. "The Bermuda Triangle Mystery Delusion: Looking Back after Forty Years." *Skeptical Inquirer*, December 2015. skepticalinquirer.org/2015/11/the-bermuda-triangle-mystery-delusion/.

Loxton, Daniel, and Donald R. Prothero. *Abominable Science! Origins of the Yeti, Nessie, and Other Famous Cryptids*. New York: Columbia University Press, 2015.

Montgomery, J. Randal. "Abducted! Scientific Explanations of the Alien Abduction Experience." *Skeptic*, December 27, 2022. skeptic.com/reading_room/abducted-scientific-explanations-of-alien-abduction-experience/.

Naish, Darren. *Hunting Monsters*. London: Arcturus, 2017.

Nickell, Joe. *The Science of Monsters: Tracking the Real-Life Creatures*. Monster House LLC, 2024.

Taylor, Richard. "Coming Soon to a Field Near You." *Physics World*, 2011. iopscience.iop.org/article/10.1088/2058-7058/24/08/35.

United States Department of Defense. "Report on the Historical Record of U.S. Government Involvement with Unidentified Anomalous Phenomena (UAP)." The Department of Defense All-Domain Anomaly Resolution Office, February 2024. media.defense.gov/2024/Mar/08/2003409233/-1/-1/0/DOPSR-CLEARED-508-COMPLIANT-HRRV1-08-MAR-2024-FINAL.PDF.

Scan the QR code below for additional sources:

INDEX

A

accidental awareness, 184–185
Advanced Aerospace Weapons System Application Program (AAWSAP), 171–173
Advanced Aviation Threat Identification Program (AATIP), 171–173
Air Force, 165, 166, 168, 169, 170, 171, 174, 180
aliens, 161, 162, 177–186, 194, 195, 203. *See also* unidentified flying objects (UFOs)
All-Domain Anomaly Resolution Office (AARO), 174
All Souls trilogy (Deborah Harkness), 80
almas, 110
American Academy of Sleep Medicine, 185
The American Journal of Ophthalmology, 52
ancestor worship, 22–23
Andreasson, Betty, 182–183
animism, 22, 25
apophenia, 41, 63, 65, 133
Arecibo Radio Telescope, 191
Aristotle, 24
Arnold, Kenneth, 164–165, 169
Associated Press, 110, 111, 164, 165
Athenodorus, 24–25
auditory apophenia, 63
Augustine (saint), 27
Australian Sheep-Goat Scale (ASGS), 39
Australopithecus genus, 118
Aztec culture, 26

B

Banks, Sir Joseph, 201
bears, 121–122
The Beast of Bray Road: Tailing Wisconsin's Werewolf (Linda Godfrey), 93
Beast of Bray Road, 93
belief questionnaires, 39
Benadryl Challenge, 159, 202
Berlitz, Charles, 151
The Bermuda Triangle (Charles Berlitz), 151
Bermuda Triangle, 150–156
The Bermuda Triangle Mystery: Solved (Larry Kusche), 153
Bethel, Brian, 147
Biddle, Kenny, 69–70
Bigelow Aerospace, 172
Bigelow, Robert, 172
Bigfoot, 107–122
Bigfoot Field Researchers Organization, 121
bipolar disorder, 45
black-eyed kids (BEKs), 146–149
Blackmore, Susan, 183
Blagojevic, Petar, 76–77, 80
Bloody Mary, 139–142, 144–145
bogeyman, 98–102
Bonaparte, Napoleon, 99
BooBuddy, 71
Bower, Doug, 190, 191
Brazel, W.W. "Mac," 169
Bridgewater Triangle, 152
Buggy Men, 99
Bugis pirates, 99
burials, 21–22, 23, 25, 79, 83–84
Burns, John W., 107
Burns, Robert, 142
Byzantine Empire, 96

C

calomel, 50
Campbell, Alex, 129
Capron, John, 188
Caputo, Giovanni, 144, 149
carbon monoxide (CO), 48, 52, 185–186

catalepsy, 89
Catherine Howard (queen), 34
catoptromancy, 142
Center for UFO Studies (CUFOS), 167
Chabris, Christopher, 43
Chapman University, 31
chindi, 25
Chorley, Dave, 190, 191
Christianity, 27, 39, 41, 92
CIA (Central Intelligence Agency), 167
cihuateteo, 26
Civil War, 29
Clancy, Susan A., 184
clinical lycanthropy, 96–97
cognitive style, 35
cold spots, 61
Cold War, 164, 166
Coleman, Loren, 152
Committee for Skeptical Inquiry (CSI), 69, 126
Condon, Edward, 168
Cretaceous period, 134
Crew, Jerry, 111
"critical lure" word, 184
crop circles, 187–192
cross modulation, 63

D

Daily Mail newspaper, 132
"The Deadly Bermuda Triangle" (Vincent Gaddis), 151
decomposition, 68
delusional misidentification syndrome (DMS), 96
Department of Defense, 162, 171–172, 173, 174
Devil's Triangle. *See* Bermuda Triangle
Diagnostic and Statistical Manual of Mental Disorders (DSM), 96
The Disappearance of Flight 19 (Larry Kusche), 153

double exposures, 59
dowsing rods, 67
Dracula (Bram Stoker), 80
Dunning, Brian, 147
Dyatlov Pass, 202

E

Early Dynastic period, 23
Early Modern Period, 92
earthquakes, 135, 156, 200
electromagnetic fields (EMFs), 51, 53, 68, 69, 70, 71
electronic voice phenomena (EVP), 62–63, 64, 71
Elizondo, Luis, 173–174
Elk, Michiel van, 42
Encounter (Kelly Cahill), 195
Epic of Gilgamesh, 90
Epicureans, 24, 161
Epicurus, 24, 161
epilepsy, 45, 89
Estes Method, 65, 66
extra-sensory perception (ESP), 39
extraterrestrial hypothesis (ETH), 163, 175

F

Fabulae (Hyginus), 90
false memory syndrome, 184
Fata Morgana, 165
Fire in the Sky (movie), 195
flashlight trick, 64
Flight 19, 150–151, 153–154, 155
Flight 370, 154
Flückinger, Johannes, 80, 83
flukes, 8
"flying saucer nests," 188, 190
Forrest, David V., 184–185
Fox, Kate, 30
Fox, Maggie, 30, 31
Foxon, Floe, 121–122
Frankenstein; or, the Modern Prometheus (Mary Shelley), 103, 201
Frank's Box, 65–66
French, Chris, 33
Friedman, Stanton, 170
full-bodied apparitions, 47
Fuller, John G., 182

G

Gaddis, Vincent, 151
galvanism, 103
Ganz, Tomas, 85
Georgian Rooms, 34
Gibbs Bridge, 158
Gigantopithecus blacki, 117–118
Gimlin, Bob, 112, 113
Godfrey, Linda, 93
Goodall, Jane, 107
grave goods, 21–22
Great New England Vampire Panic, 86
Greek culture, 24
Grusch, David, 173

H

"Halloween" (Robert Burns), 142
hallucinations, 40, 45–46, 47, 48, 53, 54, 84, 185–186, 202
Hampton Court Palace, 34, 36
Hanako-san, 143
Hanal Pixan, 26
Harkness, Deborah, 80
Harrison River Valley (British Columbia), 107
Haselhoff, E.H., 192
Hat Man, 202
Haunted Gallery, 34, 36
"haunted" locations, 15–16, 33, 49, 51, 55, 200
Haunted Mansion ride (Disneyland), 60
health tonics, 50
hedgehogs, 189
Heironimus, Bob, 116
Henderson, Paul, 180
Henry VII, 94
Henry VIII, 34
Herodotus, 90
Hill, Barney, 179–182, 183, 185, 186
Hill, Betty, 179–182, 183, 185, 186
hobgoblins, 99
hominids, 107, 113, 118, 120
Homo erectus, 118
Hopkins, Budd, 183, 185
Houdini, Harry, 55
Houran, James, 37–38, 47
Humboldt Times newspaper, 111

Hunting Monsters: Cryptozoology and the Reality Behind the Myths (Darren Naish), 133
hurricanes, 155
Hyginus, 90
Hynek, J. Allen, 167
hypertrichosis, 95–96

I

Ice Age, 135
ideomotor effect, 67
inattentional blindness, 43–44, 60
indigenous people, 118
infrared light, 61
infrasound, 51, 53
The Interrupted Journey (John G. Fuller), 182
Inverness Courier newspaper, 130

J

Jack-o'-Lantern, 28
Jacobs, David, 183, 185
Jane Seymour (queen), 34
Jones, James Earl, 182
Journal of Parapsychology, 34
Julia set, 191

K

Keel, John, 125
King Kong (movie), 131
King, Stephen, 55, 200
Knudsen, Eric, 100
Koenigswald, Ralph von, 118
Korff, Kal K., 171
Krantz, Grover, 118
Kusche, Larry, 153, 155

L

La Llorona, 26
Lancre, Pierre de, 92
Lange, Rense, 37–38
Levengood, W.C., 192
livestock mutilations, 97, 124
Loch Ness Monster, 128–135
Long, Greg, 116
loup-garous, 92
Lucretius, 24
lycanthropy, 90

M

MacDonald, John, 129
Mackay, Aldie, 129
Mackay, John, 129
Mack, John, 183
Maclean's magazine, 107
The Making of Bigfoot (Greg Long), 116
Mallette, Mary, 123, 124, 126, 127
Mallette, Steve, 123, 124, 126, 127
mapinguari, 110
Marcel, Jesse, 171
Mary Tudor, 141
Mayan culture, 26
Medina, Richard, 175–176
Meldrum, Jeff, 113
mental health, 40, 45–46
mercury poisoning, 50
Mesopotamia, 23
Metamorphoses (Ovid), 90
methane hydrate, 156
Metoh Kangmi, 110
Meyers, Stephanie, 80
Miccailhuitl (Great Feast of the Dead), 26
Miccailhuitontli (Little Feast of the Dead), 26
Middle Ages, 92
Milwaukee Depth, 154
mold, 49
MonsterQuest television show, 126–127
Moore, Patrick, 188
mortsafes, 79
The Mothman Prophecies (John Keel), 125
Mothman, 122–127, 136
mountain gorillas, 120
The Mowing-Devil: or, Strange News Out of Hartford-Shire, 187–188

N

Naish, Darren, 133
NASA, 162, 174
National Investigations Committee on Aerial Phenomena (NICAP), 180, 186
Nature journal, 188
Navajo people, 25
Navy, 150, 172, 173, 176

Neuri tribe, 90
neurologic disorders, 45–46
Newme, 102
New York Times newspaper, 171
Nickell, Joe, 126–127
Night of the Living Dead (movie), 103

O

The Official Loch Ness Monster Sightings Register, 132, 133
orbs, 58–59
Ouija board, 67
Overlook Hotel, 55
Ovid, 90
Ovilus, 70
owls, 126

P

Paole, Arnod, 78, 80
Paranthropus genus, 118
Para.Science, 51
parasomnia, 47
pareidolia, 41–42, 58, 60, 61
Parkinson's disease, 46, 89
Parsons, Estelle, 182
Parsons, Steve, 51
patterns, 40–41
Patterson-Gimlin Film, 112–116
Patterson, Roger, 112
"Patty," 112–116
Pausanias, 90
Pepper's Ghost, 59–60
perception, 40
Persinger, Michael, 53
photos, 29–30, 42, 57–60, 100, 117, 120, 132, 133, 162, 170, 178
plague, 86, 99
Plato, 90
Pliny the Elder, 90
Pliny the Younger, 24, 25
Point Pleasant Register newspaper, 123
poisoning, 50
poltergeists, 38
Poppy, Carrie, 48
porphyria, 88, 95–96
postmortem photos, 29–30
post-traumatic stress disorder, 45

power of suggestion, 200
prehistoric burials, 21
Project Blue Book, 166–167, 168, 180
Project Grudge, 166, 167
Project Mogul, 170–171
Project Sign, 165–166, 167
Proxima Centauri, 175
pseudoscience, 14
psychedelic drugs, 50
psychokinesis, 39
psychological priming, 37
puberty, 98
Puerto Rico Trench, 154
purgatory, 27, 28
putrefaction, 83–84

R

rabies, 87, 95
radio frequency (RF) interference, 63
rapid eye movement (REM) sleep, 47
Reid, Harry, 172
REM Pods, 69–70
resurrectionists, 79
Riekki, Tapani, 41
Robertson Panel, 167
Roe, William, 108–109, 111, 115, 130
Rogers, Shane, 49
rogue waves, 155
Roman culture, 24
Romero, George, 103
Roswell Army Air Field (RAAF), 169–170
Roswell Daily Record newspaper, 170
Roswell Morning Dispatch newspaper, 170
Roswell, New Mexico, 169–171
Royal College of Anesthetists (London), 185

S

Saint Lawrence Agency, 178
sasq'ets, 107
sasquatch, 107–122
Savanovic, Sava, 82
Scarberry, Linda, 123, 124, 126, 127
Scarberry, Roger, 123, 124, 126, 127
schizophrenia, 45, 86, 89
scientific method, 14–17, 70

séances, 30, 31
seizures, 45
Sennert, Daniel, 95
Serbia, 76–78, 80, 82, 83, 87
Shackleman, Mark, 93
Shelley, Mary, 201
The Shining (Stephen King), 55, 200
Silver Bridge, 125
Simon, Benjamin, 181, 182
Simons, Daniel, 43
single-axis EMF, 69
skepticism, 35, 58
Skeptoid podcast, 147
Skinner, B.F., 63
Skinwalker Ranch, 172
sleep paralysis, 47, 84, 101, 185, 202
Slenderman, 100
Smith, Robert L., 125
Society for Psychical Research (SPR), 30–31, 63
Spicer, George, 130, 131, 132
spirit board, 67
Spirit Box, 65–66, 70
"spirit photographs," 59
Spiritualism, 30–31, 55, 59, 67
Spooky Science Sisters, 9
Stanley Hotel, 200
St. Lawrence, Mike, 178
Stoker, Bram, 80
strange face illusion, 149
Sts'ailes people, 107
Stübbe, Peter, 97
suggestion, 37–38
Sumerian culture, 23
Sunghir site, 22
Survey of American Fears, 31
Sykes, Brian, 121

T

Talbott, N.P., 192
Tandy, Vic, 51
Tapanuli orangutans, 120
Tasmanian Tiger, 201
Taylor, Charles C., 150, 153
Taylor, Richard, 192
temporoparietal junction (TPJ), 45–46
Test Your Knowledge
  alien abductions, 195, 203
  cryptids, 137, 201–202
  "haunted" locations, 55, 200
  monsters, 103, 201
  urban legends, 159, 202

Thalbourne, Michael, 39
thalassophobia, 128
thermal imaging, 61
"three young anglers" sighting, 128–129
thylacines, 201–202
Today tabloid, 190
Toire no Hanako, 143
Tower of London, 34
toxic substances, 50
trinitrotoluene (TNT) area, 123, 124, 125, 127
Troxler fading, 144
tuberculosis (TB), 86
Twilight series (Stephenie Meyer), 80

U

The UFO Incident (movie), 182
unidentified flying objects (UFOs), 161, 162, 163–177, 188, 190. *See also* aliens
Usenet newsgroups, 146

V

vampires, 76–89
Venus, 177
verbal transformation effect, 63
Victorian Era, 29–31, 50, 59, 131
videos, 43, 57, 58, 59, 115, 117, 133, 148, 149, 159, 162, 171–172, 173
Völsunga Saga, 91

W

Wallace, Ray, 111
Wallace, Wilbur "Shorty," 111–112
Walton, Travis, 182
werewolves, 90–98
West, Adam, 124
West, Mick, 173
Westrum, Ron, 185
Wetherell, Ian, 132
Wetherell, Marmaduke, 132
Wilmer, William, 52
Wilson, Robert K., 132

Winchester Mystery House, 200
Winchester, Sarah, 200
wind vortices hypothesis, 191–192
The Wisconsin Werewolf, 93
Wiseman, Richard, 34, 36
witchcraft, 92, 141, 142
The Wolf Man (movie), 91
World Wildlife Fund, 156

Y

yeren, 110
yeti, 110
YouGov survey, 32
yowies, 110

Z

zombies, 103, 201

ACKNOWLEDGMENTS

First and foremost, we would like to thank our listeners and followers, without whom this book wouldn't have happened, especially Rage Kindelsperger of The Quarto Group who birthed this whole idea! Also, thanks to the wonderful folks at Evergreen Podcasts for hosting our show and our audio editor, Jessica Andrade of Ear Honey.

The paranormal podcasting community, including both skeptics and believers, has been a welcoming, fun group to be a part of and we would like to recognize a few people we've collaborated with and learned from over these last few years. This includes (in no particular order): Kenny Biddle, Karen Stollznow, Tyson Kemp, Allison Kirkpatrick, Brian Regal, Annelise Baer, Sara Head, and many others who have appeared as guests or helped us along the way.

Last, but not least, special thanks to our editor, Elizabeth You of The Quarto Group, who helped us shape our vision for this book and put up with our many, many questions. Your encouragement and gentle guidance were invaluable throughout this process.

Meagan: I'd like to thank my husband, Steve Ankney, and daughter, Alice, for their love, support, and patience while I went down the rabbit hole to write this book. Also, thanks go to my parents, Curt and Katie Bosket, for letting me watch *The X-Files* when I was probably too young and always making sure I had amazing Halloween costumes.

Paige: Thank you to my close friends and family, whose support is unwavering and who have stuck with me through every panicked phone call or text over the last several months (you know who you are).

I'd like to thank my parents for making sure I always had the most original, handmade Halloween costumes and for letting me explore horror as a child. My love of Halloween and the spookier things in life started with you.

Lastly, a special thanks to my best friend and husband, Elliot, who was our third set of eyes for the initial drafts of the book in front of you today and who took care of our dog and our home while I locked myself away several days at a time.

ABOUT THE AUTHORS

Meagan Ankney is a geologist by training, a chemist by trade, and a lifelong Halloween enthusiast. In 2020, she took her love for all things spooky and her passion for science communication to the podcasting world, when she founded the *Spooky Science Sisters* podcast with her ride-or-die sister-in-law, Paige Miller. When she isn't podcasting, making spooky science videos, or writing, Meagan enjoys playing cozy games, reading fantasy novels, and exploring her home state of Wisconsin with her husband and daughter. *Spooky Science* is her first book.

Paige Miller, a chemist by training, spends her time working as a safety professional and EHS graduate student. A lover of Halloween and horror since childhood, Paige enthusiastically joined her sister-in-law, Meagan Ankney as the cohost of the *Spooky Science Sisters* podcast. A first-time coauthor of *Spooky Science*, Paige works and writes out of Wisconsin. Her free time is spent playing with her dog and exploring the great outdoors with her husband.

© 2025 by Quarto Publishing Group USA Inc.
Text © 2025 Meagan Ankney and Paige Ankney

First published in 2025 by Wellfleet Press,
an imprint of The Quarto Group,
142 West 36th Street, 4th Floor,
New York, NY 10018, USA
(212) 779-4972
www.Quarto.com

All rights reserved. No part of this book may be reproduced in any form without written permission of the copyright owners. All images included in this book are original works created by the artist credited on the copyright page, not generated by artificial intelligence, and have been reproduced with the knowledge and prior consent of the artist. The producer, publisher, and printer accept no responsibility for any infringement of copyright or otherwise arising from the contents of this publication. Every effort has been made to ensure that credits accurately comply with information supplied. We apologize for any inaccuracies that may have occurred and will resolve inaccurate or missing information in a subsequent reprinting of the book.

Wellfleet Press titles are also available at discount for retail, wholesale, promotional, and bulk purchase. For details, contact the Special Sales Manager by email at specialsales@quarto.com or by mail at The Quarto Group, Attn: Special Sales Manager, 100 Cummings Center Suite 265D, Beverly, MA 01915 USA.

10 9 8 7 6 5 4 3 2 1

ISBN: 978-1-57715-479-2

Digital edition published in 2025
eISBN: 978-0-7603-9302-4

Library of Congress Control Number: 2024948968

Group Publisher: Rage Kindelsperger
Editorial Director: Erin Canning
Creative Director: Laura Drew
Managing Editor: Cara Donaldson
Editor: Elizabeth You
Art Director: Scott Richardson
Interior Design: Maeve Bargman

Printed in China